PROSTHETIC
MAKE–UP ARTISTRY
FOR FILM AND TELEVISION

PROSTHETIC
MAKE-UP ARTISTRY
FOR FILM AND TELEVISION

CLARE RAMSEY

THE CROWOOD PRESS

First published in 2019 by
The Crowood Press Ltd
Ramsbury, Marlborough
Wiltshire SN8 2HR

www.crowood.com

British Library Cataloguing-in-Publication Data
A catalogue record for this book is available from the British Library.

ISBN 978 1 78500 591 6

Acknowledgements
The Monster Makers (www.monstermakers.com)
Crownbrush (https://crownbrush.com and https://crownbrush.co.uk)
RBFX Studio (rbfxstudio.com)
Models: Thomas Groholski and Philip Moffett

Typeset by Jean Cussons Typesetting, Diss, Norfolk

Printed and bound in India by Parksons Graphics

CONTENTS

INTRODUCTION

The greatest achievement was at first and for a time a dream ... Dreams are the seedlings of realities.

James Allen, *As a Man Thinketh*

NOTE FROM THE AUTHOR

I am a self-taught artist from Northern Ireland. When I first took an interest in the world of prosthetic artistry it seemed to be a rare art form. In fact I only discovered it might be a viable career when DVDs replaced old VHS tapes and we were introduced to the goings on behind the scenes of the movies we had just watched. I was captivated!

I began my professional career as a high school teacher in Ireland but I longed to work in the film industry. James Allen's words were on the wall of my classroom and inspired me every day to keep striving towards my dream of becoming a prosthetic make-up artist.

In the beginning I worked in my own little bubble, seeking whatever information I could from books and DVDs. I set about practising techniques and working on my portfolio. I had no one to ask for advice or guidance, so books were my main source of education when it came to learning about prosthetics.

When I finally moved to London I was incredibly grateful to the artists I met and had the opportunity to work with. They were very generous with their knowledge and helped make me the artist I've become today.

The techniques shown in this book are only one way to achieve the results you see, as there are many ways to achieve similar results. I'm still learning new techniques every day and don't think you ever really stop learning in this industry. My hope is that I can pass on some of my experience with the aspiration that it might inspire and encourage others who share this passion and who may perhaps be interested in pursuing prosthetic artistry as a hobby or career.

Before we get into the finer details of this book, let's draw attention to one of the most important aspects: health and safety.

If you intend to tackle any of the techniques shown in this book you must possess an excellent awareness of safety in all aspects of your work.

In the world of prosthetic artistry you will encounter all sorts of weird and wonderful chemicals, glues, solvents, paints and so on, all of which have been used for years and are designed with the professional make-up artist in mind. However, you should be aware of the hazards each one carries and use it according to the manufacturer's instructions.

DISCLAIMER

All tutorials, techniques, information and processes described in this book are provided in good faith. The health and safety of readers attempting anything described in this book are the sole responsibility of that person and/ or persons. *You alone* are responsible for any damage or injury you cause to an individual or property.

The author Clare Ramsey, the publishing company Crowood as well as all suppliers and sponsors of materials will not be held liable under any circumstances.

It is important that you understand and practise standard safety precautions. This is paramount when working with the materials described in this book.

Data Sheets are available on request for all materials and are available directly from the suppliers. Contact them and request Materials Safety Data Sheets. Educate yourself and follow the prescribed precautions.

You must be over 18 to use the hazardous materials depicted in this book, otherwise you will need the supervision of a responsible adult. These materials are extremely dangerous and flammable and must only be used in a well-ventilated area. Please keep them safely out of the reach of children and pets.

Your own health and safety, as well as those you will involve in the processes described here, are of the utmost importance.

HOW TO USE THIS BOOK

This book aims to provide some insight into the role of a prosthetic make-up artist within the film and television industry. It will also teach you a variety of different practical techniques that you can implement and interpret into your own personal characters.

The book has been broken down into three character designs. Through the use of photos, diagrams and explanations you will be shown a series of techniques and how each has been utilized to build a complete character at the end of each segment.

Each character uses slightly different techniques and practical applications.

You have the option to follow along with each technique and arrive at your own character, or you can dip in and out of the chapters taking each one as a standalone lesson.

THE CHARACTERS

Gelatine Goblin character

This section will take you through the entire process of making a prosthetic character from scratch:

- Life casting half a human face
- Sculpting a new face on a life cast
- Making a one-piece mould in silicone and plaster
- Making prosthetic-grade gelatine
- Making gelatine ears
- Realistic painting
- Realistic hair work
- Punching hair
- Hand-laying facial hair
- Gelatine application
- Prosthetic removal

Foam Latex Centaur character

This section will show you how to take a generic foam latex piece and transform it into your own character:

- Using the computer as a design tool
- Airbrushing, including the parts of an airbrush
- Painting foam latex
- Applying foam latex

Foam Latex Lion character

This section illustrates how you can transform a generic prosthetic appliance, enhancing the design using character teeth and hair to give it a unique look:

- Making personal novelty teeth
- Casting your own teeth
- Sculpting new teeth
- Painting the teeth
- Fantasy animal hair work using faux fur
- Self application

PART 1

GETTING STARTED

1

WHAT IS PROSTHETIC MAKE-UP?

Prosthetic make-up involves the application of specifically designed make-up appliances to change the appearance of an actor or performer in some way. These are made in a variety of flexible materials and are glued to a person's face and/or body.

They are designed to move in a realistic fashion and are primarily used to help tell a story as they allow extreme changes to be made to a performer. Some examples of these extreme effects include ageing, disease, fake pregnant bellies, adding or losing weight, fantasy and horror creatures. The possibilities are limitless.

This book is mainly concerned with prosthetic make-up artistry for film and television, however the art of prosthetics isn't limited to this medium. It reaches as far as print and editorial work, theatre, cosplay and live-action role play. It is even used to train medical practitioners by simulating casualty effects.

Prosthetic artists often work with surgeons to provide realistic body parts that they can practice delicate procedures on.

THE VARIOUS ROLES OF A PROSTHETIC MAKE-UP ARTIST

Those interested in this craft have a number of options as there are many processes involved in working with prosthetics. Usually at a professional level the process begins in a prosthetic workshop, within which there may be many hands and minds that contribute to the prosthetic appliances an actor wears.

Some artists are based in workshops and deal mostly with the design and manufacture of the appliances, while others work as application artists on TV and movie sets, applying and maintaining the prosthetics on actors and performers throughout the filming shoot. Other prosthetic artists divide their time between workshop and application jobs.

As well as manufacturing prosthetics appliances, workshops also manufacture fake bodies in the likeness of actors that can be used in

CONCEPT TO APPLICATION

A prosthetic appliance is developed from thought to reality within the workshop infrastructure

> Workshop managers meet with producers, writers and directors to discuss the requirements of their story

↓

> Designers come up with character designs, including a few variants, until a decision has been made for the final look

↓

> A life cast is made of the performer

↓

> Sculptors create a three-dimensional design on the new head casts

↓

> Mould makers produce moulds of this new design in order to run many duplicates

↓

> Technicians cast these out in a flexible material, creating the prosthetic appliances

↓

> Art finishers paint the prosthetic appliances and add hair if required. The appliances are then carefully packed and delivered to the on-set team.

Usually a brand new piece will be required every day an actor is working as each one is destroyed during the removal process, so the workshop will continue to turn out these appliances until the total amount is reached.

Eventually the appliances are handed over to the make-up department on a film or TV set where they are applied by skilled prosthetic make-up artists individually or as part of a duo team.

situations where, for example, death or injuries need to be simulated. Workshops also make masks of actors' likenesses to be worn by stunt performers in film and TV, as well as simple quick-change prosthetics and masks for theatre. Every job is different and the requirements are always unique.

WORKING AS AN ON-SET PROSTHETIC MAKE-UP ARTIST

When you work as a prosthetic make-up artist on a film or TV set your job involves applying and maintaining prosthetics on a performer. Prosthetics can take anywhere from two to six hours (or longer) to apply. Due to these long application times you will usually be applying the pieces working as a team with another prosthetic artist. Each artist works on one side of the face, crossing over where necessary.

Having two people working together like this reduces the application time, making the process more comfortable for the performer. It oddly becomes like a strange prosthetic dance as both artists work in tandem to create the character. Thus you will need to be able to work well in a team environment.

Depending on the type of prosthetic pieces, however, you won't always be working in pairs, so you need to be competent and efficient at applying prosthetics alone as well as part of a team.

In an on-set environment prosthetic artists fall under the umbrella of the make-up department, but they are generally separate from the regular make-up team as they often require a specific set of skills and equipment, not to mention the time they need to do their work.

It is the role of the regular make-up team to deal with all the beauty and corrective make-up on the other cast members. They will also handle any small wounds such as scars and cuts, using the two-dimensional prosthetic transfers you will learn about in Chapter 3. These are generally made by prosthetic artists and then handed over to the regular make-up team.

OUT-OF-KIT EFFECTS

Another technique regular make-up artists employ is simply to create the wounds using a method called 'out-of-kit effects'. Loosely translated this involves applying scar material or collodian directly to the actor's skin to simulate scars, cuts and small wounds. It is a fast and effective way to create the appearance of injuries, but due to its one-of-a-kind nature it has the disadvantage of never quite looking exactly the same if it has to be repeated. When a make-up must be repeated on a different day the make-up team relies on continuity pictures taken on the previous occasion. These photos have to be copied as closely as possible to recreate the look.

This is why the lesson on flat moulded prosthetics in Chapter 3 is such an important skill to learn, since it will save you a lot of time when it comes to repeating these small designs.

Out-of-kit techniques are also utilized by prosthetic make-up artists when a creature has minor changes, small cuts and wounds that can be applied quickly and then removed as necessary. The appearance and stages of an injury, for example, can change a lot in a day's filming. You need to be ready to jump in with a quick solution when needed. This topic will be investigated further later in the book.

Generally prosthetic artists deal with the specialized make-ups and creature characters that can't be done within a regular make-up department. They work closely with each other as often both elements are required on one performer. There is generally a make-up designer and a separate prosthetic designer, but this isn't always the case and it largely depends on the requirements of the job and the available budget.

Some artists work solely as prosthetic make-up artists, while other regular make-up artists do prosthetics as well. The more skills you have, the more employable you will be.

A TYPICAL DAY FOR A PROSTHETIC MAKE-UP ARTIST

4 am: arriving at work.

04:00 (or earlier): Arrive at work

Prosthetic artists need a few hours to get an actor ready, time that is allocated before the rest of the film crew arrives. An average prosthetic application time is three hours, during which they will prep the actor's skin, then apply and paint the prosthetic appliances.

The entire day will be set out on a schedule known as a call sheet. This is a detailed document that explains the plan of action for the day, indicating when the actor will arrive and what scene number they will film. It also informs the team which other members of the cast are involved in the same scene, as well as any special influences that may be needed, such as an actor having a stunt double or needing fake injuries.

07:00: Finish make-up

While the prosthetic artist is in the last stages of the make-up, the rest of the film crew will have arrived and set up for the day, ready to begin filming as soon as all the actors are ready.

Good time-management skills are essential, as it's imperative that each prosthetic artist works to the time frame allocated, since delays could hold up filming. Delays could potentially cost a production company a lot of money as they disrupt the carefully planned day.

When the prosthetic application is complete the actor will leave the make-up chair and finish getting on the rest of their costume. This will give the prosthetic team time to clean up their work station and pack up a small kit to take to set that will be used to maintain the make-up throughout the day. There may also be an opportunity to get some food at this point (meals are usually provided on film and TV sets).

07:30: Maintain the make-up

The prosthetic artist will then travel to the set with the actor, taking the maintenance kit with them. This on-set kit allows the artist to preserve the make-up during the day, making sure edges don't become unglued and that everything, includ-

PRODUCTION OFFICE 123 Little Lane Big Town Welly WI56 7PU	*Made Up Movie*	Director	Name
		Producers	Names
		Executive Producers	Names

<u>**CALL SHEET NO**: 03 Tuesday 30th October 2018</u>

NO EATING OR DRINKING ON SET! NO MOBILE PHONES ON SET!
Crew Minibus will s/by @ The Home from Home Inn & depart for unit base @0655
PLEASE NOTE BREAKFAST WILL BE SERVED @LOCATION.
A MINIBUS WILL FERRY CREW FROM UNIT BASE TO LOCATION FROM 0720
RUSHES VIEWING IN THE PRODUCTION OFFICE ON WRAP TBC

Line Producer: Name Production Manager: Name Production Co-ordinator: Name		**Breakfast available**	**07:15**
2nd AD: Name 3rd AD: Name Crowd Assistant Director: Name Floor Runner: Name		**UNIT CALL** **Lunch @Location for** **Est. Wrap**	08:00 13:00 18:30
Loc Manager: Name Asst Location Manager: Name		Sunrise: 07:16 Sunset: 16:58	
Unit Manager: Name			
		UNIT BASE **Center Field** **Springfield Road** **Welly** **WL67 H765**	

Weather Today: Mostly Cloudy Max Temp of 12° Low of 10° Wind SW 9Mph

Sc	LOCATION	SCENE DESCRIPTION	D/N	Pgs	CAST #'S
75	The Corin Mill 5 -7 Corin St	INT ABANDONED WAREHOUSE *Brian & Sam listen to the radio as Kieran interrogates a man*	D 18	5/8	1,3,10,11,47
77	The Corin Mill 5 -7 Corin St	INT ABANDONED WAREHOUSE *Brian challenges Merl*	D 18	1 1/8	1,3,10,11,47
119	The Corin Mill 5 -7 Conin St	INT IRA WAREHOUSE *Brian briefs the crew (inc dialogue from Sc 120/1/2/3/4)*	D 40	3/8	1,3,6,10,30
103	The Corin Mill 5 -7 Conin St	INT WAREHOUSE *Sam makes a plan*	D 32	2/8	1,3
			Total Pages: 2 3/8		

Typical call sheet.

ing the paint, remains fresh. It's common to film all the wide shots first and do the close-ups later in the day. The prosthetic artist must ensure the make-up looks good throughout the day. Before each scene is filmed you will be given a brief opportunity to check the edges and general appearance of the prosthetics. The actor may not be required for every single scene, so you can take these opportunities to fix any major flaws, if necessary.

Working on a professional truck.

The call sheet is carefully followed as the entire filming crew work throughout the day, checking off each planned scene. Prosthetic artists need to pay close attention to the call sheet as it indicates any changes they might need to make to their character during the day: they may, for example, be bloody in one scene but need to be cleaned up for the next. Often these quick changes need to be conducted on set, so the artist must have everything needed to facilitate this. There will also be a meal break during this time.

19:30: Clean up

After a long day filming it usually takes somewhere between 30 minutes to an hour to carefully remove the prosthetics from the performer. This means that the prosthetic team is often one of the last departments to leave in the evening. When this is complete they set up their station for the next working day and then go home to sleep, ready to repeat it all the following day.

WHAT IT TAKES TO WORK AS A PROFESSIONAL PROSTHETIC MAKE-UP ARTIST

Working as a prosthetic make-up artist in the film and television industry requires an infinite

amount of skills. There are the obvious technical requirements, such as artistic ability, an eye for fine detail and the ability to mix and blend colours seamlessly, but there is also the important responsibility for the performer's safety while working within a disciplined unit.

Correct attitude

Aside from the mandatory artistic ability you need to have the correct attitude to work in this profession, which is seldom as glamorous as folk think.

You also need to be prepared to work incredibly long hours, and perhaps only manage to get a few hours' sleep at night. Little sleep can make people cranky and sometimes more susceptible to illness. You need to look after yourself, trying to get enough rest, eating well and staying healthy.

You might also find yourself working in trying environments, which might mean sweltering heat on one job and sub-zero temperatures on the next, or spending long hours in the wind and rain. Having the right attitude means not complaining constantly, as it makes situations worse and makes your day even longer.

It can be a challenging job at times, but it is indeed a very rewarding one that will enrich your life in many ways.

Working on location in Iceland with actor Luke Neal.

Those who choose this career are artistic, passionate and driven, and they generally have a good sense of humour. The humour is mandatory, as it will make the long days seem that little bit shorter.

Be a team player

You will work closely with many age ranges and different personalities for extended periods of time. You will need good interpersonal skills to communicate effectively.

Ultimately you need to be an excellent team player. Remember you are a small cog in a giant wheel and cogs are easily replaced, so be professional and invaluable to the rest of your team and you'll continue to get work.

With a positive attitude you will do well in this industry. Don't engage in gossip or negative dialogue. Respect the people you work with, no matter their rank.

Be prepared to make sacrifices

The career of a film and television prosthetic artist can be varied and rewarding as no two jobs are alike. You will meet interesting people and perhaps you will be given the opportunity to travel to exciting places.

Choosing a career as a make-up artist, however, isn't without sacrifices. You may often work weekends and even have to leave your friends and family for months at a time, missing important family occasions, when the job requires you to work in another country. As a career it has pluses and minuses, but it is more often than not aptly described as a vocation.

Working as a freelancer

As a self-employed freelance you will find yourself worrying when and where your next job will come from. You will need to be proactive about seeking out employment, as not only will you need to learn the practical skills required, you will also need to network with other artists to find out about upcoming work. You should keep your financial affairs in order as work can be sporadic and you may have to budget your earnings effectively for less busy times. Remember to keep all your receipts and learn how to manage taxes, invoices and paperwork.

You will need to keep up to date with current techniques and add new skills to your repertoire. As your skills develop you will make yourself even more employable.

In conclusion, if you are truly passionate about this craft you will find that this feeling far outweighs any negatives. Those who choose to be a prosthetic make-up artist do it simply because they love it and couldn't imagine doing anything else. There is definitely a sense of pride and achievement when you see your work in a movie theatre or on a TV screen, which is acknowledged as your name rolls up in the end credits.

2
RESEARCH, EQUIPMENT AND SETTING UP

In Chapter 1 we looked at the attributes of a prosthetic artist. This chapter considers practical skills and how to go about research, as well as the equipment needed and how to set up your work area.

TOOLS FOR RESEARCH

Prosthetic characters take their influences from all kinds of sources. When you are given the task of designing a prosthetic character there are a few sources you can call upon.

Nature: Look around you! There is a multitude of textures that you can see and touch. Trees, rocks, plant life, animals, fish and birds have some of the richest sources of inspiration that you can draw on as an artist. Look at the colour combinations of plants, fish and reptiles or the direction the fur lies on a dog's face and the structure of its teeth. Nature is bursting with inspiration.

Man-made artefacts: Again there is an infinite range of textures that you can draw upon, such as smooth and shiny metal, electrical circuitry, and the multifarious colours and textures selected for plastics. Take a moment to look around the environment in which you are sitting and see if any influence there could be translated into a prosthetic creature.

Anatomy: Study it. If you can grasp the basis of a human skull and the underlying muscle you will be a better sculptor, your prosthetics will look more realistic and they will move more naturally. If you know about human anatomy you can exaggerate and translate that knowledge into a creature, pushing the boundaries of a character to the extreme. Look at photos of pumped-up bodybuilders for how their muscle tone stands out or, at the other extreme, how the skin stretches over the bones of those who are seriously underweight. Learn about symmetry and asymmetry. No face is 100 per cent symmetrical, so study your own face and jawline, and then look closely at other faces.

People: Study ethnic characteristics, how people age and how their skin folds and creases. Look at skin tones, pores, freckles, tattoos, age spots, pimples and scars. Reproducing these elements can help you bring realism to your sculpture and paint job. Gather pictures of people from photos and books. Look at the wealth of information about fashions through history.

Medical books: Seek out photos of wounds, scars, skin afflictions and various injuries that appear in medical books and online sources as they can help bring realism to your work.

Art books: Draw inspiration from studying all

forms of art, including the old masters, modern art, comic book art and sculpture.

Work by other prosthetic artists: Observe other artists' work in film and TV, as well as their own personal work. It's often difficult to come up with a new and interesting design as it all seems to have been done before, but you will gain much inspiration from looking at other people's work, both professionals and amateurs alike. Don't plagiarize it, just appreciate and get inspired to creature your own design.

REFERENCE SOURCES

The Internet is by far one of the most valuable tools you have at your disposal. You will find endless sources of inspiration. It can provide you with pictures, videos and historical data as well as instructional text and demonstrations. You can store images of your work in the form of websites and photo storage accounts.

Social media has made the world a little bit smaller and also more accessible. You can easily look up the work of other effects artists on sites using various search engines. You can follow their work and they in turn can follow you. There are many personal art and photo storage display sites that provide access to a vast range of inspiration, allowing you to build banks of pictures that you can refer back to at will.

Libraries provide you with books on most topics ranging from old to new. Art reference libraries are particularly useful. Libraries aren't just for books, however, as they also hold archives of old newspapers, magazines, photographs and DVDs. The librarians who work there can point you in the right direction quickly and effectively.

There are a few magazines aimed specifically at film make-up and prosthetic artists. You will find these are both educational and inspirational.

From fantasy to documentary, historical to horror, film and television will continue to inspire prosthetic artists. It is the medium for which the craft was intended. It contains the creatures we love and loathe and remains the motivation for many artists.

COLOUR THEORY

This knowledge is one of the most important tools you can possess. In order to be a successful prosthetic make-up artist you will need to have a good eye for colour and be able to effectively blend prosthetic appliances into a performer's skin or match the colours of a pre-painted prosthetic. You will also have to mix gelatine or silicone to match as closely as possible a performer's skin tone, or perhaps you will be required to paint a fantasy creature and will need to know about complementary or neutral colours. Whatever the application, it's mandatory to have a good understanding of colour theory and how to mix colours successfully.

Colour theory is a vast topic so this chapter will break it down into simpler terms covering the fundamentals. There are lots of helpful resources available in art books and online that will help you understand the concept further.

Primary colours.

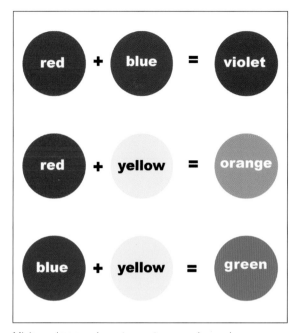

Mixing primary colours to create secondary colours.

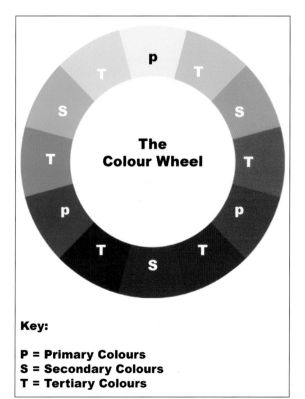

Key:

P = Primary Colours
S = Secondary Colours
T = Tertiary Colours

The colour wheel illustrates the process of mixing colours.

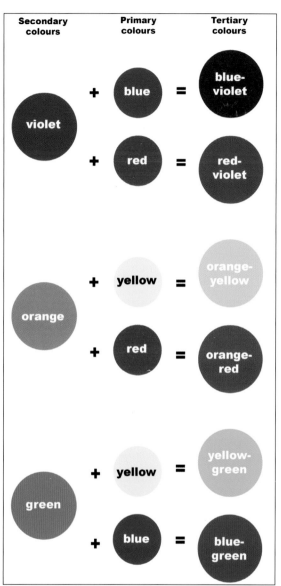

Mixing secondary and primary colours to create tertiary colours.

Primary colours: All colours that exist are derived from the three primary colours: red, blue and yellow. These are pure pigments and cannot be made from any other colour.

Secondary colours: By mixing two primary colours in equal amounts you will make new secondary colours.

Tertiary colours: By adding equal amounts of the new secondary colour with an equal amount of the original primary colour you will achieve a tertiary colour.

Colour wheel: The process of mixing colours, known as colour theory, is best displayed in the form of a colour wheel.

Shading

The addition of black or white to the chosen colour results in what are known as tones and tints, respectively. This alters the tonal quality of the colours, making them into darker or lighter shades.

Tonal shading can be applied to other colours and is an essential skill when it comes to painting. The ability to shade from light to dark and vice versa is something that will repay careful practice.

It's also worth noting that colours can be further altered by diluting them. Depending on the medium used, you can alter the translucency and opacity of the colours by using water or a solvent. This is helpful when it comes to painting

Neutralising Colours

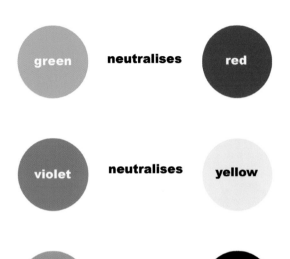

Certain colours can be neutralized by following these rules.

prosthetics as diluted washes of colour are often utilized to give a more translucent effect.

Neutralizing colours

Some colours can be used to neutralize the effect of others. This is particularly useful if you need to cover tattoos, for example. You first need to use an orange colour to neutralize the blue/black lines of the tattoo before applying another layer of colour that matches the person's skin tone. The diagram given here demonstrates which shades of colour work best to neutralize the other colours shown.

You will only become more competent and confident by practising and playing with colours. You may find it helpful to make your own colour wheel. It can also be a useful exercise to make a skin chart that you can photograph up against

Shading and Tone

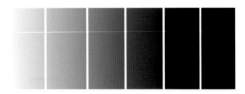

An understanding of shade and tone and how to achieve a seamless transition from light to dark is a useful skill to have.

an actor to provide a more accurate colour reference for their skin tone. Some artists have excellent colour memory and can mix colours that match exactly, while others like to measure out their colours accurately to ensure an exact match every time. Keep a notebook handy when you have to mix colours, particularly for large batches of colour, as this will make life a little easier. Familiarize yourself with different colour mediums and the array of paints and pigments available to prosthetic artists. If you are starting out and are on a budget, simple cheap acrylic paints will help you learn the theory of colour before you move on to more expensive paints or inks.

BUILDING A KIT

At the beginning of each tutorial there will be a detailed list of materials and tools that will be required, but the following list of items can be used for most prosthetic applications. They will provide a good starting point if you are trying to build a kit to work as a prosthetic make-up artist.

Empty bottles and containers are useful for decanting smaller quantities of liquids like IPA. A funnel will help prevent spillages and a spritzer bottle is a must when working with alcohol-activated ink palettes.

A basic hair kit is helpful when applying bald caps and styling hair.

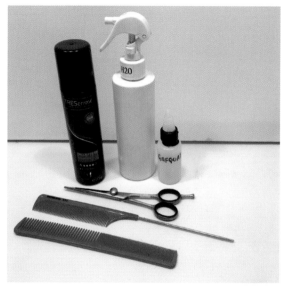

A basic hair kit is essential when putting hair under a bald cap, or for styling character hair.

Empty bottles and containers are useful to decant products.

You will require an array of sponges in different textures.

Sponges are used to blend in the edges of prosthetics and also to paint them. It can help to have a number of different textures.

Powder puffs are essential to remove the tack of certain glues and paints. Use them with translucent powder to eliminate shine.

Among the most useful tools to have for application are long tweezers, which are great for pulling out edges that are difficult to get to with your fingers, for example around the eyes. Tweezer

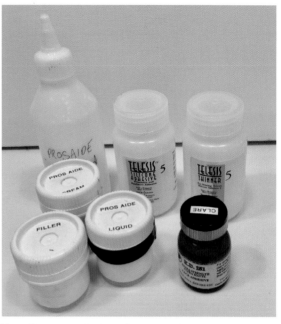

You will need a selection of glues and fillers in your kit in various consistencies.

Powder puffs, colourless translucent powder, a bowl and brush will help you eliminate sticky edges.

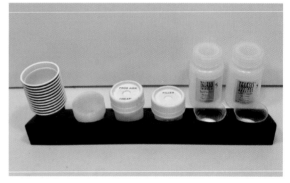

Glue holders are useful as the glue is expensive. This tool will allow you to decant the product into smaller cups and will help avoid spillages.

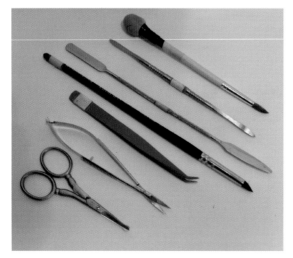

Some of the most useful application tools.

scissors and safety scissors are a must for tasks like trimming edges. Spatulas will help you fill in the edges with filler. You will find that all of these tools will make life much easier.

There are many glues to choose from. The ones illustrated are among the most popular. They can be expensive, but if you are starting out and on a budget you may find smaller sample sizes of each one.

Skin preparation items help you cleanse and protect the actor's skin when applying adhesive and appliances.

You will need a small battery shaver and medical cleaning spray for when you need to remove face and body hair prior to application.

Since the glues for prosthetics are expensive it's best not to use it directly out of the pot in case it spills. More importantly for hygiene purposes, decant it into a smaller cup and place this in a holder to prevent the cup toppling over.

You will need to look after a performer's skin by cleaning it with astringent and protecting it with barrier foam. Vaseline is carefully applied only to the eyelashes as it prevents them sticking together.

An electric face razor and beard trimmer, as well as medical grade cleaning equipment, are also useful to have in your kit as they will give a closer shave.

A selection of shaving skin care products will help care for the actor's skin.

You may need to remove facial or body hair prior to applying prosthetics. The tools shown above include medical clipper hygiene spray. You should always be clean and considerate, and let the performer see that you are using it. You should always strive to keep your equipment in impeccable condition, especially these items. Shave powders can help eliminate redness and razor rash.

Hygiene sprays are available to help keep your kit sanitary. Hand sanitizer is also useful to have, especially on set.

Hand and make-up sanitizers are essential items to have in your kit to keep everything sanitary.

You will go through a lot of disposable items. Individual eye drops are also important to have in your kit, making sure that they are safe to use with contact lenses.

Artist's palettes provide a good means of mixing colours. Both disposable ones and the traditional style can be used.

Fans are useful to have during application and also on set to keep the actor cool. They also help to eliminate fumes from paint, glues and other substances.

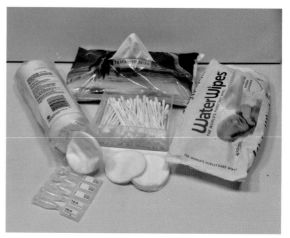

You will find that you go through hundreds of disposable wipes. Make sure you have a supply for your workplace as well as on set.

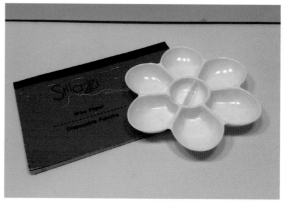

As well as regular artist's palettes, disposable palettes are useful when mixing colours.

You can start building up some colour palettes in your kit. Alcohol inks are a staple and another must is a good matt eyeshadow palette.

Vinyl gloves (not latex), respirators and dust masks should always be in your kit to keep you safe.

A hand-held fan and a battery or USB powered one are great for helping the actor to stay cool. They are also useful in warding off fumes.

Take safety seriously. A good respirator mask will be needed that can deal with heavy paint fumes. You will also need some dust masks and vinyl gloves.

You will need a number of paint palettes, including a selection of alcohol-based inks as this is the medium most commonly used to paint prosthetics.

A small hair punching kit will allow you to create realistic hair.

Brushes made with synthetic hair are best for applying glue.

Paint texture brushes.

A hair punching kit is useful if you need to do hair work on a prosthetic (for more details see Chapter 7).

You will need a selection of glue brushes in various shapes and sizes. Angled brushes are useful for getting into tight spots around the eyes, nose and mouth.

You will also need paintbrushes of various types and sizes for painting textures.

When you are starting, don't run out and get everything all at once as this can get very expensive very quickly. You can gather up your kit gradually and look for items that can multitask. As you become more experienced you will identify the items that are most useful.

SETTING UP THE WORK AREA

Prosthetic make-up will always need a suitable environment in which to do it. It can get messy, so choose somewhere suitable. You will need the following:

- A table
- A chair
- A mirror
- Notebook and pencil
- Protective coverings for the floor and table (if necessary)
- A protective cape or covering for the performer
- A good source of natural light or daylight bulbs
- A clock
- A fan

RULES TO FOLLOW

The following guidelines are something that you should implement every time you embark on a practical make-up application. Make them part of your routine.

Patch test

Always do an adhesive patch test for safety. Put a small blob of glue behind the performer's ear or on the wrist, preferably a few days before application is planned. If there is no sign of an adverse reaction you will be able to continue applying the make-up. If a reaction or irritation occurs, *do not* use the products and seek medical attention.

Hygiene

Wash your hands before touching the performer. Always make a point of letting them see you washing your hands, as this will help put them at ease and inform them that you are hygienic and professional. If you sneeze, cough or blow your nose in the middle of an application, stop and re-wash your hands. You should also use hand sanitizer. These are basic common sense rules of hygiene, yet people often forget them.

Cleanliness

I cannot stress enough that you should keep your kit spotless. I'm often shocked at the lack of hygiene among make-up and prosthetic artists. Clean all your make-up brushes after use on a performer. Never use the same brush on another artist without first thoroughly cleansing it. Eye infections and cold sores (herpes) can easily be transferred from person to person. Don't forget the sanitizing spray when using an electric shaver/trimmer to remove facial or body hair prior to an application. Make sure the performer sees you spray it with hygiene spray before use. It should also be thoroughly cleaned after every use. Most people, however, prefer to shave with their own beard trimmer.

3

MAKING FLAT MOULDED PROSTHETICS

Before we get into the three character designs we are going to start by making some two-dimensional or flat moulded prosthetic appliances. This is a useful skill as it can be used to make small prosthetic appliances for use on regular actors when they require a cut or wound. You may also use these small appliances on your prosthetic character if they sustain an injury.

This invaluable technique has been around for some time. The development of new materials such as silicone has made possible an extremely effective method for manufacturing prosthetics that can be stored in the mould and applied very quickly when required.

The end result seen on film and television screens is almost never shot in the correct sequence. An actor may be inside a room and in the next scene they have walked outside, but these two areas could be in different locations filmed months apart. The actor, however, must look exactly the same so the audience cannot tell it wasn't a sequential shot.

In order to achieve this the make-up department adopts a process called continuity, by which detailed photos and notes are made recording the scene number, time of day, location, costume, hair and make-up. This then has to be copied exactly so everything looks exactly the same.

The following technique is utilized by professional make-up artists when they have to apply the same make-up look repeatedly to a performer, such as a cut, a scar or perhaps a diseased element to their skin. The injury must always be the same shape and in the same place.

This technique allows you to make multiple moulds of the same design and have a fresh appliance each day to apply to the performer. Prosthetic transfers are also known as Pros-Aide transfers or bondos.

Materials and tools

- Oil-based clay
- Sculpting tools
- Lighter fluid or naphtha. This is flammable and should only be used in a well-ventilated area and wearing a respirator
- Talc
- Clay extruder (optional)
- Hairdryer
- Ultra 4 epoxy parfilm. Vaseline can be used as an alternative
- Acetone
- Cheap chip brush (cut down)
- Cotton tips
- Artist's spatula, or metal scraper
- Artist's brush for use with the lighter fluid
- Mixing sticks
- Plastic mixing container
- Scales
- Ziplock bag (big enough to cover scales)

Flat prosthetic materials: sculpting tools and clay.

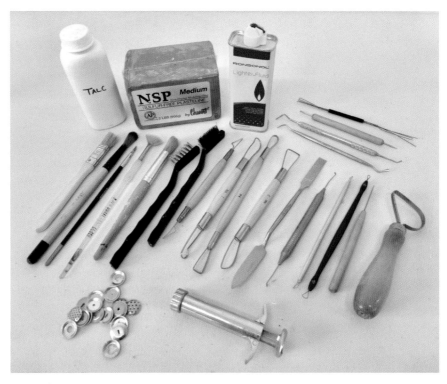

- Vinyl gloves (not latex)
- Vaseline
- Airbrush and inks (optional)
- Respirator mask for use with lighter fluid and cap plastic
- Cap plastic (acetone-based)
- Pros-Aide cream transfer material (pre-bought or home-made)
- Dressmaker's pins
- Scissors

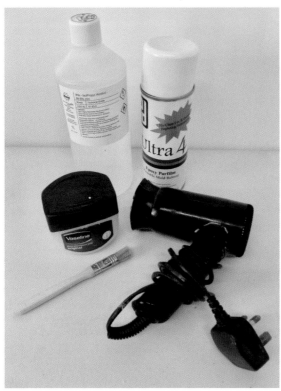

Flat prosthetic materials: hairdryer and mould release.

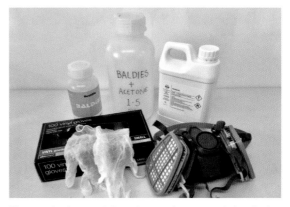

Flat prosthetic materials: safety equipment and chemicals.

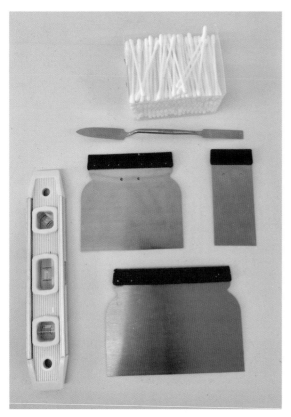

Flat prosthetic materials: scrapers.

- IPA – Isopropyl alcohol (99%)
- Spirit level (optional)
- Flat surface to sculpt on (must be texture-free)
- Powder brush
- Thickened Pros-Aide cream or store-bought prosthetic bondo (not to be confused with the automotive body filler of the same name)

GETTING STARTED

In this demo we are going to do a very simple sculpt to demonstrate this technique. There really is no end, however, to what you can so with this method. You can, for example, make features such as scars, cuts and bullet hits. You could even make simple facial prosthetics, as long as you keep the sculpt reasonably thin.

Step 1: A clay extruder is a handy tool that can be used to make things go a little faster. It can be taken apart and comes with various shaped dies that fit in the end of a barrel-like tube. It is then filled with clay and the plunger is inserted. When this is engaged the extruder pushes the clay out of the end through the die and creates a long piece of clay like spaghetti. Variants with a twist plunger are much easier to use with this oil-based clay as it is quite hard. One way of making

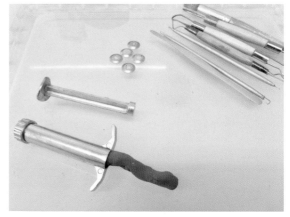

Clay extruder.

Warming the extruder.

The extruded clay comes out like spaghetti.

it easier to use the plunger is to heat it up with a hairdryer, but take care that the metal doesn't get too hot to handle.

Step 2: Next you will need to find a flat surface such as a piece of glass, perspex or a large ceramic tile, which needs to be completely smooth and non-porous, as you will be pouring liquid on it in the form of silicone. In the example shown here the lid of a plastic box is being used. The extruded worm of clay is arranged into the required shape, such as a vein. If you find that the clay does not stick to the surface on which you are sculpting, rub on a very thin layer of Vaseline and the clay should stick better, allowing you to work in finer detail.

Lighter fluid can be used to clean up the edges of the veins.

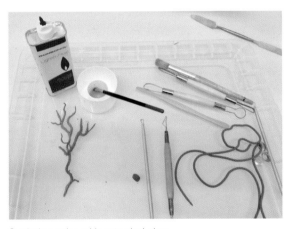

Sculpting veins with extruded clay.

Close-up of the veins.

Lighter fluid (naptha), applied with a paint-brush, is used to give the sculpt a smooth pointy edge. If you use too much fluid the clay will turn to a slurry, so you only need a little. Lighter fluid should always be used in a well-ventilated area with a respirator mask.

You can also use the lighter fluid with a cotton tip to clean up in-between and around your sculpt.

Step 3: Once the lighter fluid has evaporated off the sculpt, you can then dust it with a little talc. This will absorb leftover lighter fluid and help eliminate any little balls of clay that may have gathered.

Talc helps smooth out the veins after lighter fluid has been used.

Step 4: Continue using this method to fill your board with sculpts. You could add different designs such as scars, small wounds or bullet holes. You will then have a stock of moulds that you can use as you wish.

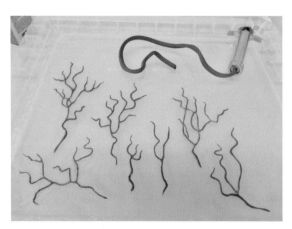

Making more veins for future use.

Step 5: The sculpts should now be flooded with silicone in order to capture the design and make a negative impression of it. In order to do this without the silicone spilling everywhere you will need to build a retaining wall around the sculpts. This is again a little quicker and neater when using the clay extruder, this time with a square die.

The wall should be securely fixed to the sculpture base, again using a little Vaseline to help the clay adhere better.

It's very important that there are no gaps in your clay wall, otherwise when you fill it with silicone it will leak out and make a huge mess that will ruin all your hard work. To make it secure, go around the outside edge with a tool or your finger and rub the clay into the board. This will seal it sufficiently to prevent any leaks. As long as the

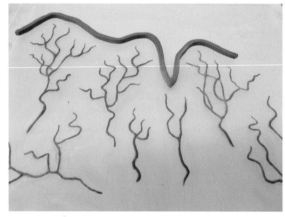

Building a clay wall around the veins.

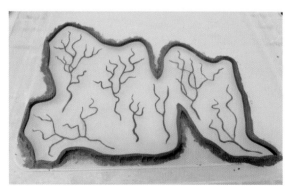

The completed clay wall.

Close-up of the wall.

Silicone equipment.

wall looks good on the inside it doesn't matter what the outside is like. Your priority is to prevent silicone leaking out.

Step 6: You will now need to gather your silicone equipment and prepare to pour it into your mould. Both platinum-based and tin-based silicones are available and within these two types there is a myriad of different brands, all of which have different applications. It can get rather confusing, but the companies who sell silicone are very helpful and have a wealth of information and video tutorials to help you learn more about the applications of the different materials.

A platinum silicone will be used for this demo as it gives you more options. The type used here is PlatSil 7315 from Mouldlife, which has two components (A and B) that must be mixed at a 1:1 ratio. The main advantage of using this product is that it cures clear, which lets you see the placement of the final prosthetic on the skin.

You could also other platinum silicones by Mouldlife, such as PlatSil Gel 10 or PlatSil Gel 25, or alternatives such as SORTA-Clear and Dragon Skin from Smooth-on.

Silicone can get very messy so you need to work in a suitable environment. It's also imperative that you have separate cups and mixing sticks to decant the product into. Anything that touches the A component must be kept

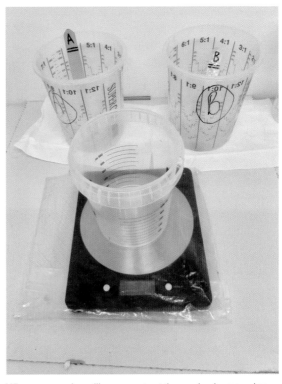

When measuring silicone, protect the scales by covering them with a ziplock bag.

separate from the B component, otherwise they will become contaminated and start to cure. Get into the habit of working neatly and label everything to avoid cross-contamination.

Step 7: Some silicones that require a 1:1 mix ratio don't need scales, since you simply put equal amounts in a measuring cup. However it's much better to get into the habit of using scales for more accuracy. A tip is to cover your scales using a ziplock bag. Silicone is messy and this will protect your scales from any accidental drips. Just remember to zero out the scales with an empty cup for ultimate accuracy.

Step 8: The instructions on some silicone packaging state that degassing is recommended. This involves putting the two mixed components into a small vacuum chamber and drawing out the air bubbles in the silicone. Unless you are in a prosthetic workshop it is unlikely you will have access to one. Air bubbles, however, can

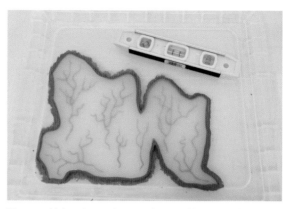
Use a spirit level to make sure the moulds are perfectly flat.

be eliminated using the high pour technique, which involves holding the mixture high above the mould and letting a thin steady stream trickle down into the mould. This actually stretches out the air bubbles. You will still get a few bubbles, but they can be popped with a pin or by blowing forcefully on the surface of the mould, although you should be wearing goggles if you do this as it can splash.

Another tip for making a uniformly flat mould is to use a spirit level to make sure the table and board are flat.

Some bubbles are still present in the silicone shown here in the mould. There should be no problem with a few bubbles as long as they aren't on the layer closest to the sculpt. They will

High pouring the mixture to help stretch out the bubbles.

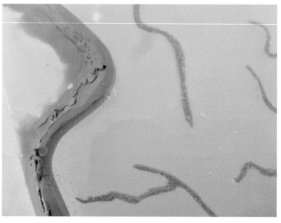
This view indicates the thickness of poured silicone that you should aim for.

Use a sharp tool to lift the edge of the cured silicone mould.

Use some release spray to help release the final vein transfer.

generally rise to the top if you tap underneath the table, and you can pop them as they rise. Using a clear curing silicone is extremely helpful when positioning the piece on the performer. It will aid continuity immensely as you will be more likely to put it in the same place each time. More opaque moulds tend to require some guesswork, but a useful tip is to line them up with a freckle or mark on the performer's skin.

PlatSil 7315 takes a little longer to cure than some other silicones and is best left overnight. If you leave a little of the mix in the cup you can tell when it's completely cured.

Step 9: After you remove the silicone from the mould, carefully cut around each shape with scissors, keeping away from the edges of the design. You will now have individual moulds.

In order to make sure the prosthetic transfer you make comes away from the mould easily, spray on some Ultra 4 epoxy parfilm release, used on its own, or you can be doubly safe by adding a thin layer of Vaseline. In fact you could use the Vaseline on its own, massaging a good amount into the mould, leaving it for 15 minutes to be absorbed by the silicone and then lightly wiping off the excess, making sure to leave a fine coating in the mould.

A fine layer of Vaseline will also serve as a release agent.

Step 10: The cap plastic should then be thinned with a little acetone. Since both cap plastic and acetone are extremely flammable, this should only be done in a well-ventilated area and when wearing a respirator mask. When you purchase cap plastic it comes as a thick concentrated liquid. In this state it's too thick to use alone and you will achieve better edges by applying a few thinner layers rather than one thick layer. It is possible to airbrush it and this will ultimately give you the best edges. You can also paint it on if you don't have an airbrush.

A popular brand of cap plastic is Baldiez from Mouldlife, which is available as both regular Baldiez and Super Baldiez. The main difference is that regular Baldiez is thinned with acetone, while Super Baldiez is thinned with isopropyl alcohol. Always take care and read the labels when working with materials. Similar brands available include Bentley cap plastic and Q-Ballz from Smooth-on.

For this demo the cap plastic is thinned in a ratio of two parts solvent to one part cap plastic (in this case it's regular Baldiez, so the solvent is acetone). Brush the cap plastic mix in various directions using a flat synthetic brush and build up two or three layers, not too thick, allowing each layer to dry. It's best to allow it to dry naturally as a hairdryer can cause the material to bubble up, ruining your piece and meaning you'll have to start again.

If you wish to airbrush the cap plastic, the ratio is about four parts acetone to one part cap plastic. If you find that the cap plastic tends to 'web' when you apply it by airbrushing, add some more acetone.

The thickness of the cap plastic can be tested using a dressmaker's pin to gently lift the cap plastic in an inconspicuous area. It should lift away and have a solid membrane, not one that's webbed and disintegrating. You don't want it to be too thin or too thick and it takes practice to determine the correct level of thickness. You can't rush the process of making these pieces as you need to give the solvent time to evaporate or

'flash off' the piece. If you move on too soon you will find that attempting the next step will ruin the cap plastic layer.

Step 11: The pieces are made from a prosthetic transfer material. This is essentially a thickened Pros-Aide cream adhesive that can be bought from make-up suppliers. Some types are tinted but clear is more versatile. When you first pour it into the mould it is a milky white colour, but when cured it dries clear. It can be tinted to the desired colour with a small amount of acrylic paint, but you should do a test first as it may dry lighter or darker than you anticipated.

Scraper tools are then used to scrape the mixture over the mould. This fills the negative space, giving you the prosthetic required.

A wide selection of tools can be used to scrape the material. An artist's palette knife in metal or plastic is useful, while Japanese scrapers have

Scraper tools and thickened Pros-aide cream (bondo) coloured with acrylic paint.

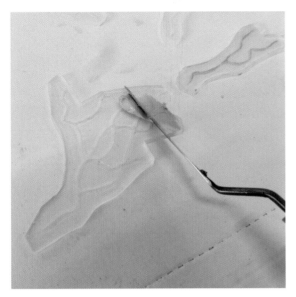

Scraping the bondo into the moulds.

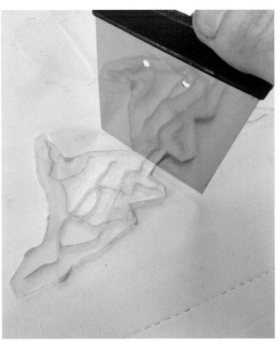

The excess product should be removed with the scraper tool. The rest will remain in the vein shape.

long flexible blades that work really well. You can even get good results from a plastic or metal ruler, as long as it has a straight edge.

The palette knife can also be used to decant the Pros-Aide material. You should put out a lot more than you need because the cap plastic layer is really delicate and you will want to scrape as little as possible. In fact you should think of

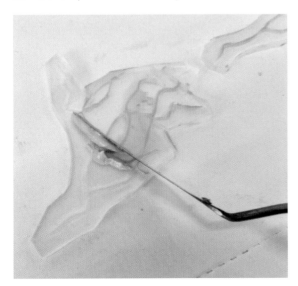

Use the spatula to spread the material across the whole mould.

it as more of a sweep, trying to fill the mould in just one or two passes. The aim is to leave the Pros-Aide material in the recess while the edges are left clean. Any excess that you don't want left on the mould can be gently wiped away with a dampened cotton tip.

Any excess material scraped off can be put back into the tub, which should be kept sealed at all times as it will dry out and spoil. Make sure to thoroughly clean all of the scrapers as the material will dry and be more difficult to remove later.

Step 12: Give the pieces plenty of time to dry. Prosthetic transfers are made from a thickened water-based adhesive. In order for them to fully dry the water needs to evaporate out of them completely. This takes some time: the thinner the sculpted piece, the quicker it will cure and vice versa.

You must always make these in advance. If you are lucky you may find that when removing the first pull of cured silicone from your mould it comes out cleanly without damaging the sculpt. There is then nothing to stop you from running duplicate negative moulds.

Filled prosthetic transfer moulds can be put in a food dehydrator to help things along, but you must keep it on a low setting as too much heat on uncured Pros-Aide transfers can lead to bubbling, just as it does on uncured cap plastic.

When the pieces are fully cured you can blend off any excess cap plastic around the sculpt using acetone, which will give the appliance a seamless edge when applied.

Step 13: You are now ready to apply your Pros-Aide transfer. Clean the area you are going to stick it to with a little IPA or astringent. When this is dry, position your mould and then press

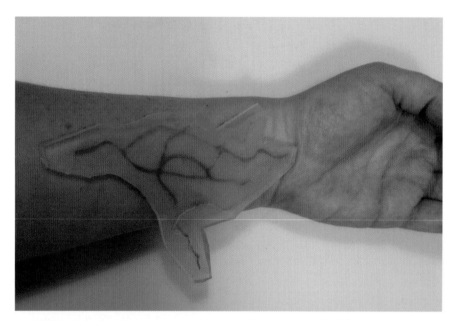

Place the mould on the skin.

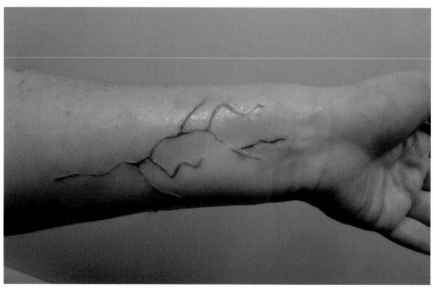

When you press and peel the silicone mould back the vein will self stick to the arm, it will have some shine to it at this point.

down firmly on the back of the mould for a few seconds. The advantage of using PlatSil 7315 is apparent here as you can see exactly where the underlying vein prosthetic is positioned.

Carefully peel back the edge of the mould and check to see if it has begun to release. Since these are made from an adhesive they are self-sticking, which is why they are so quick to apply.

When the mould is fully removed the appliance should be stuck securely to the skin. It will look a little shiny at this point. The shine can be eliminated using a no-colour powder, pressing it in and brushing it off.

Step 14: The finished piece can now be embellished with paint or you can simply leave it as it is.

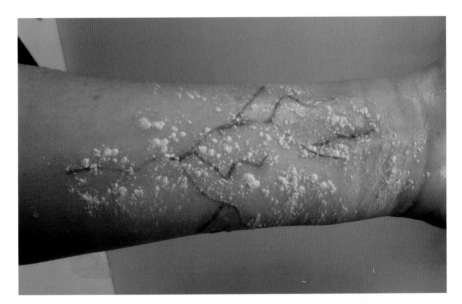

Powder the piece with no-colour powder to eliminate shine.

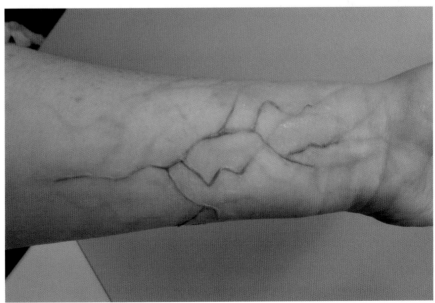

You can use an airbrush to soften the look of the veins by adding some more in varying translucences.

PART 2

GOBLIN CHARACTER: FROM LIFE CAST TO APPLICATION

4

LIFE CASTING

Using prosthetics to change someone's appearance can only be achieved by adding prosthetic appliances onto a person's face and body. When we want to make someone look overweight, for example, adding to their face is the logical thing to do.

If, however, we want to make them look gaunt or ill, or as though they have lost weight, this can also be achieved by adding something. This, however, is where the artistry and technicalities of making and applying prosthetics come together.

Using carefully sculpted pieces with edges that slope at subtle angles to melt seamlessly into the skin, we can fool the camera and, it is hoped, an audience that the transformations taking place before their eyes are real. A poor sculpt, a bad paint job or an edge that has unglued itself from the performer's face ruins the illusion. We are yanked out of the story and snapped back into reality and our eyes will continue to look for imperfections. All these elements have to be in place for a prosthetic character to be believable.

In this part of the book we will investigate how someone's appearance can really be altered using three-dimensional prosthetics. Here you will observe how a prosthetic character comes into being. Everything for this character has been made from scratch, so you will come to realize how all prosthetics are born from a piece of clay.

By the end of this section you will see how all the different techniques shown come together to create a Goblin character. If you are interested in pursuing prosthetic artistry as a career, a character such as this will show a prospective employer how you are able to implement a variety of skills successfully.

WHAT IS LIFE CASTING?

If you want to make a prosthetic that will fit your performer exactly and move along with their own facial muscles, you will need to take an impression of their face.

This process is known as life casting and it requires the application of a flexible impression material – in this case alginate – to a performer's face. Once it sets on the face it needs to be supported by another material, such as a plaster bandage, which will create a hard shell. When all the components have fully set the entire cast is removed, yielding a negative impression of the person's face. This is then filled with a hard material, usually plaster. When this has set and the original casting impression has been removed you will be left with an exact replica of the performer's face right down to the pores of their skin.

SAFETY FIRST

Life casting has been practised for many years. When done correctly it is a safe process, but it can also be dangerous if the people carrying out the cast don't know what they are doing. Many of the video tutorials on the Internet are misinformed and extremely dangerous. The lack of information is somewhat shocking and it's sad to think these people are sharing videos in a vain attempt to educate others.

If this is your first life cast and you are a little nervous, it might be a good idea to assist a professional first until you feel more confident. It might also be a good idea to start out with a half head, such as this demo.

It is possible to cast the entire head, creating a bust with neck, chest, shoulders and ears. This is a more advanced technique and you should have a bit more experience before attempting it: if you don't know how to divide the head sections correctly you could potentially lock someone's head in the plaster mould.

Something else I have seen online is the use of plaster, or sometimes plaster bandages, directly on the skin to make a face impression. This is never an acceptable practice. Plaster goes through a chemical reaction that causes it to heat up as it sets. You could burn someone very easily or damage their eyes, not to mention the damage you could cause to their skin.

It is of the utmost importance to read all of the instructions that come with your casting material thoroughly as these may vary slightly. Be well prepared in advance and work safely, taking both your own safety and that of your performer into consideration at all times. Remember you are working with other human beings who may be claustrophobic and anxious, or have allergies and head colds. It's never a good idea to cast someone suffering from nasal congestion. The process involves leaving only two small holes around their nostrils to breath. If they are already having difficulty breathing, then you can imagine that it probably wouldn't go so well.

There are stories of people being sick inside casts or even fainting. These, of course, are extreme cases and the subjects having the cast done probably shouldn't have gone along with it. Please remember to communicate with your performer and explain the process thoroughly, showing them pictures or videos of the process, as it may help them better understand what they are about to encounter.

Work with a partner when doing a cast, since the faster you can complete the cast and get the performer out the better. Prep your work space as well as the performer, so that cleaning up will be minimal. Never leave your performer while the materials are setting and keep letting them know you are there. Work out some hand signals before you start, perhaps one for 'I'm OK' and another for 'I need out'. It's also a good idea to

---

GOOD HABITS

Be Informed
Be Organized
Be Considerate
Be Safe
Apply this mantra to all the demos in this book, as each one is done at your own risk.

give them a notebook and pencil; they won't be able to see what they are writing, but at least they will be able to scribble brief communications or concerns.

Life casting can look and sound like a scary business but don't be put off, even though this chapter will keep reiterating the importance of safety during this tutorial. Simply be aware that this process must be done correctly. Life casting can also be a pleasant experience. In fact people getting cast sometimes describe it as 'like a weird kind of facial'. A bonus is that it's always a novelty for the performer to see their own face from an entirely new perspective.

The information captured on life casts makes them invaluable tools to you as a prosthetic artist. Study them carefully, looking at the pore texture and patterns. Look at how the wrinkles fold around the eyes, nose and mouth. Taking time to study all the details will help make you a better sculptor.

IMPRESSION MATERIALS

The two main materials used to life cast people are silicone or alginate. For this demo we will use alginate as it is much more cost-effective than silicone. Silicone has the advantage of never drying out, so multiple casts can be made from one impression. It is, however, more than three times the price of alginate.

This makes alginate a winner when you are starting out. It's fairly inexpensive and readily available at most make-up effects suppliers online, as well as at a few make-up stores and hobby shops.

Alginate

Alginate is a raw material derived from seaweed, specifically dried kelp. It is mixed with other components and sold in powder form. When combined with water and allowed to set it makes a flexible rubbery substance. Some alginates can contain silica, which is a food grade thickener. When mixed with water it is fine, but in its raw powder state it has very small dust particles that can be dangerous when breathed in. It is essential to wear a dust mask when mixing your alginate. Alginate containing silica tends to be firmer and to have a better tear strength, making it good for larger areas. It is usually mixed at a ratio of one part alginate to three parts water (again read your instructions as they may differ).

Silica-free alginate is a lot softer and tends to be more economic as it is usually mixed in a ratio of one part alginate to five or six parts water (or as instructed).

Some companies add fibres to strengthen their mix. There are different strengths available and each alginate has a different working time. The cure/set time can be delayed or accelerated by adjusting the temperature of the water: colder water will extend the working time, while hotter water will reduce the working time.

Choosing the correct alginate

Dental alginates are best left for casting teeth, as they set very quickly. Look for an alginate that has a slightly longer setting time to give you the opportunity to work with the material. You need to work it into all the planes of the face to get the best cast, so make sure you have enough

Alginate material and mixing bucket.

time to do that. Don't get one with a very long work time, either, as this will slump off as you are trying to get it to stick to the face. Those types of alginate are best used for body casts. In this demo I will be using Monster Gel TG (Traditional Grade) prosthetic alginate. It's a good general-purpose material that mixes easily by hand to a very creamy consistency. It works well with luke-warm water and gives you approximately four to five minutes working time at 26.7°C (80°F).

Test the materials

Another good habit to get into is to run a few tests on your materials. Alginate is considered skin safe, but there may be some who react differently, so you should perform a patch test on the performer. Since they will be wearing a bald cap to protect their hair, you should also test the adhesives you plan to use.

Mix a small test batch of the alginate. This is especially helpful if you are new to working with it. You need to make sure it sets well and also double-check the time it takes to cure or set. You may have to adjust the water to a cooler temperature if the test batch sets too quickly. The temperature of your environment can also influ-

ence the set time. Make sure that you are aware of the material's viability before you start covering someone's face in it.

Alginate manufacturers will help you decipher how much material you need for the cast. Some of them supply pre-made kits, which can be helpful when you are starting out. Make sure the mixing container you are using has a big enough capacity for your mix, as you need to mix it vigorously and quickly in order to get a good consistency. The countdown begins as soon the water touches the powder.

Always put your alginate powder in the container first and then add the water to the alginate. If you do this the other way around, it will result in a lumpy mix.

When you come to mix up the full batch, make around 10 per cent more than you think you will need, as it's better to have a little extra. Fresh alginate does not stick to set alginate. A product called Algislow will help with this problem, but it is better to eliminate it by making sure you have too much rather than run out.

Now that we've covered alginate in depth, let's look at the other materials you need.

CONDUCTING A LIFE CAST

Preparation

Gather all the items listed below before you prep your performer. Having everything set up in advance will make the entire process flow smoothly: once you start it will be difficult to prep as you will have wet hands.

Cut up the plaster bandages before starting. Approximately two rolls should be enough for a half face cast. Note that smaller sections will be used to help support the nose area.

It is really important to keep a spare bucket of water so you can rinse your hands. The buckets or mixing skips used here are made from a flexible material, making them excellent for this application and much easier to clean. They are

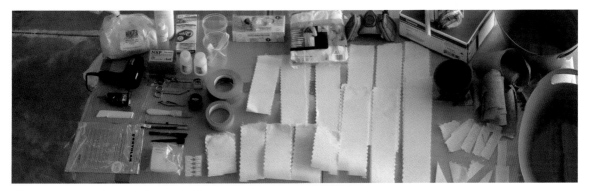

Life casting materials.

widely available in supermarkets, hardware and craft stores, as well as online. When you have finished you can let the plaster settle to the bottom before carefully pouring off the excess water. Let the remaining plaster dry off and then flex the bucket to release the plaster into the rubbish bin. Do not under any circumstance pour plaster down the sink as this will ruin your plumbing.

Flexible buckets and plaster bandage.

Materials and tools

- Alginate
- Bald cap to protect the hair (alginate sticks to hair like crazy)
- Strong-hold hair gel, such as Schwarzkopf Got2b Glued or Kryolan Gafquat, to flatten hair to the head under the bald cap
- Comb
- Hairdryer
- Glue for bald cap – Pros-Aide or Telesis 5
- Scissors
- Eyebrow pencil to draw the hairline on the bald cap. This will transfer into the cast
- Petroleum jelly
- Cotton buds or Q-tips
- Individual eyedrops (just as a safety precaution)
- Nivea face cream (optional). It's good as a release on the skin and will stop the alginate sticking to hair. Petroleum jelly also works, but Nivea is easier to clean up
- Duct/gaffer tape (optional). This can be used to secure a waste bin liner around your performer if you don't have a paper suit (these can be pricey)
- Disposable paper suits for both you and the performer, since alginate and plaster can get a bit messy. A bin bag will also work instead of a paper suit to protect the performer
- Latex or vinyl gloves

- Dust mask, to be worn when mixing alginate due to the harmful silica content
- Eye protection (goggles or safely glasses)
- Wooden mixing sticks (tongue depressors)
- Large notebook and pencil
- Plaster bandages (2–3 rolls) cut into strips in advance. Remember to prep a few smaller ones for the nose
- Burlap or hemp – to reinforce the final plaster cast
- Four mixing buckets or skips: one each for alginate, plaster, water and for cleaning your hands (remember to never put plaster down the sink)
- Strong plaster – Hydrocal and Herculite no. 2 plaster work well. Do not use plaster of Paris
- Clay – to block the nose holes on the finished life cast prior to filling with plaster
- Plastic tarp to protect the area. Life casting is messy. A tarp is also useful for covering the chair
- Clean-up materials – it might be helpful to have some clean-up items for the performer, such as wipes and towels, though it is most likely they will want to have a shower afterwards.

Make sure the chair is protected.

Choose a suitable environment

As life casting is messy, make sure to choose a suitable environment. Put down lots of plastic tarp to help protect the floor and to make clean up easier. Most professional workshops will have a special area set aside for life casting, but you will most likely have to improvise. Just remember to be respectful to the area. This can easily be achieved if you are organized and work as neatly as possible.

In the exercise shown here we are using a garage and a normal kitchen chair, which has been covered in plastic wrap to protect it.

Protect the performer

The safety and comfort of the performer must be at the forefront of your mind when life casting. Alginate and hair are never a good combination! If alginate gets in the hair it will envelop it completely and you will have to cut the hair, so protect the performer's hair at all cost. The easiest way to do this is to use a bald cap. A cheap impression cap is fine. It doesn't have to be beautifully applied with all the edges melted

TOP TIP

If the performer has long hair, the quickest technique is to put their hair in a ponytail, make a hole in the bald cap and pull the ponytail through. The ponytail can then be wrapped in aluminium foil or cling wrap to protect any exposed hair.

seamlessly as you will have to do some clean-up work on the final cast anyway, at which point you can sand off any marks left by a bald cap.

When the bald cap is in place, carefully mark the hairline using a water-based marker or water-colour pencil. This will transfer onto the final cast and can be helpful if you need to keep any prosthetics under the performer's natural hairline. Remember to protect the other hair on the face, such as eyebrows and eyelashes. These can be covered with a fine layer of petroleum jelly. You can make a life cast with facial hair even though it's not ideal, but sometimes a performer needs to keep their beard or moustache for a job they are working on. Again you need to protect the hair using a product called Cholesterol Hair Conditioning Cream, which is available from hair salon suppliers as well as some supermarkets, and is easily removed with soap and water. Nivea Creme can also be used (make sure it's the original creme in the blue tub with a screw top).

The chosen product or petroleum jelly should be placed on all hair, including any body hair that may come into contact with alginate. It's worth noting that some silicone casting products have a different set of rules when it comes to hair, but with alginate you should always use a release.

Once you have prepped both your environment and the performer it's time to get started with the life cast.

The first step is to mix up the alginate. As mentioned earlier, your work time starts running out as soon as the water hits the alginate powder, so you need to work quickly and efficiently.

You should also have carried out a test to determine how long the material takes to cure and adjusted the temperature of the water as necessary.

Carefully following the manufacturer's instructions, weigh out the powder into a dry mixing bucket. Again, always add the water to the powder, never the other way around, otherwise the resulting mix will be lumpy.

Step 1: Mix very quickly until all the powder has been absorbed by the water. As soon as this happens you can begin to apply the alginate to the performer.

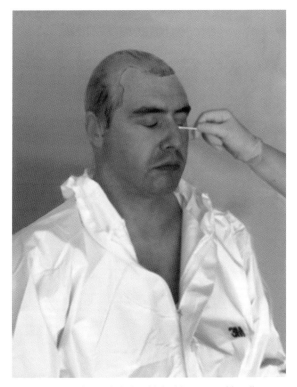

Protect the performer's hair with bald cap, put Vaseline on their eyebrows and protect their clothing.

When mixing alginate, put the powder in first and then add water.

If you add water and mix thoroughly with your hands, you can feel if there are any lumps.

Step 2: Start placing the alginate on the performer's head, beginning at the top, and spread it down around the sides of the face.

Step 3: You may find it helpful to use a disposable chip brush to work the alginate into the planes of the face. This will ensure even coverage.

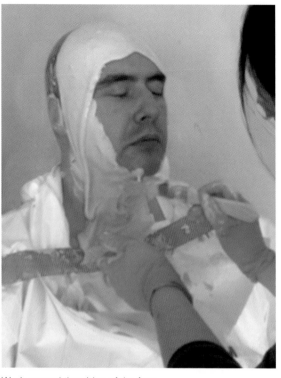

Work around the sides of the face.

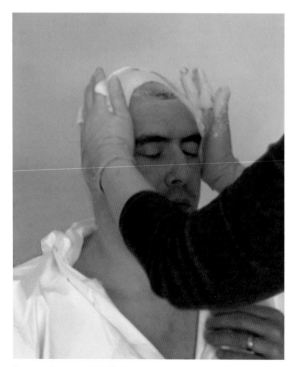

Start at the top with alginate.

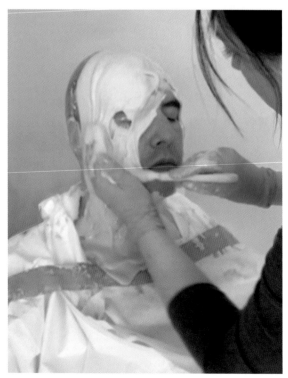

Use a brush to help working in the alginate.

Step 4: Continue spreading the alginate mixture evenly over the entire face and neck, leaving the nose area until the very end. This is more comfortable for the performer.

Step 5: Once you have covered the nose with alginate, it is extremely important to make sure you have left the nostril area clear so the performer can breathe comfortably.

Step 6: Using a wooden or plastic tongue depressor, smooth the alginate over the entire cast. This will make it easier to attach to the plaster bandage.

Step 7: At this point the alginate will have started to set. You should have already prepped the plaster bandage by pre-cutting it in advance. Using water slightly warmer than room temperature will

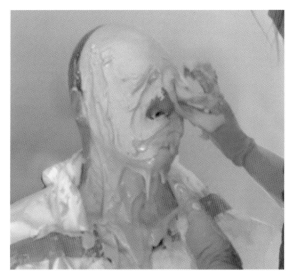

Leave the nose free until the end.

Smooth off the face cast.

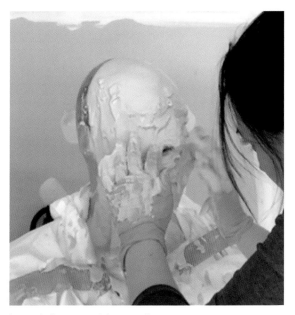

Leave holes around the nostrils.

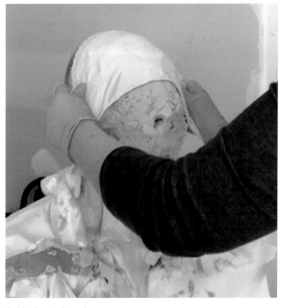

Add plaster bandage.

accelerate the rate at which the plaster bandages cure. Start laying them in place at the top of the head. They should not be too wet or too dry, as you need them just right. Hold on to the top of the strip when you dip it in water, then squeeze out excess water between your index and middle finger down the length of the bandage. This helps activate the plaster and creates a smooth strip to work with.

Step 8: Follow the same pattern with the bandages as you did with the alginate, going across the top of the head, then under the chin, and placing the rest across the face, leaving the nose to the end.

Step 9: Smooth off the surface of the bandages, making sure that all the plaster is rubbed in well. Lastly use the small pre-cut strips to reinforce the nose area, again making sure to leave the nostrils clear.

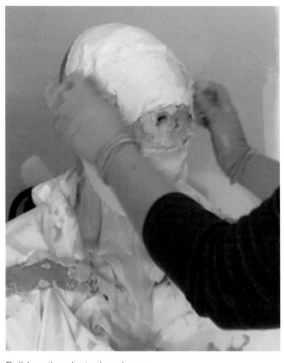

Build up the plaster bandages.

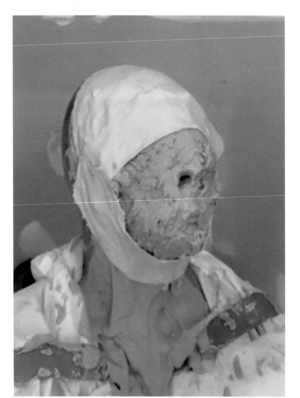

Follow the same pattern that you did with the alginate.

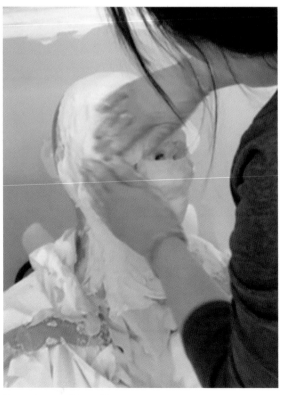

Smooth everything off.

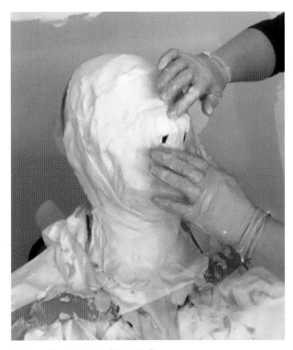

Add a strip between the nostrils.

Step 10: During the 'curing' stage you should always stay with the performer and never leave them. Use your communication system to ask if they are feeling well and explain that the final stage of the cast gets warm and heavy. As the bandages begin to cure they will heat up. As they set quickly, double-check the leftovers from your alginate mix to ensure it's fully set. Next ask the performer to wrinkle their face and pull faces inside the mould. This will help loosen the mask. Then they should lean forward and place their hands on the cast. This will ensure that it comes away from the face safely.

Step 11: You now have an exact replica of the performer's face that captures every detail, wrinkle and pore. The next step is to plug the nostril holes in preparation for making the plaster cast, as you don't want the plaster to leak out the nostrils. It is important to do this quickly as alginate can shrink. You can also add plaster bandage to the outside of the cast to reinforce this area.

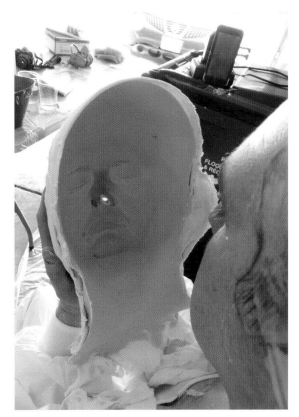

When dry the cast can be removed.

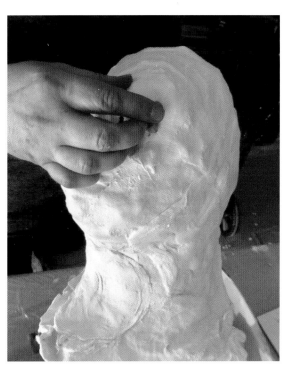

Plug the nose holes with clay.

Cover with plaster bandage.

Use a dry container when transferring the plaster into the water, employing a shaking motion to help it disperse better in the water. Continue adding the powdered plaster to the water.

You will know you've added enough plaster when a little island forms at the top of the plaster mix. The plaster will absorb the moisture of the water and you will know the mix is ready when cracks like a dry riverbed start to form.

Continue adding plaster.

Step 12: Next mix your plaster, using a flexible mixing skip to make it easier to clean. Unlike alginate, which is mixed in the opposite way, when mixing plaster always add it to the water. However much water you use, you will need to double the amount of plaster. Use something like Hydrocal or Herculite no. 2 as the cast needs to be strong (plaster of Paris is not suitable for this job).

Keep adding water until you achieve the effect of a dry riverbed.

Unlike alginate, it's better to add plaster to the water.

Step 13: You now need to mix your plaster well. Some people like to mix it by hand as it's easier to feel the lumps in the mix and break them up. It is advisable to wear gloves as the plaster can dry out your skin. Mix thoroughly until you get a smooth texture similar to Greek yoghurt.

Thoroughly mix the plaster until it is lump free.

Step 14: You are now ready to fill the cast. Make sure you have positioned it in a safe area. In order to get the best cast you should make sure it is level, which will ensure the plaster can't leak out anywhere. Another bucket and some padding are used to support the cast and keep it in the correct position. Your goal is to make sure you capture all the detail of the cast while eliminating air bubbles. The most effective way of doing this is to paint in the first layer. This is known as a splash or detail coat. Use a disposable chip brush and carefully paint an even layer of plaster, building it up as you go.

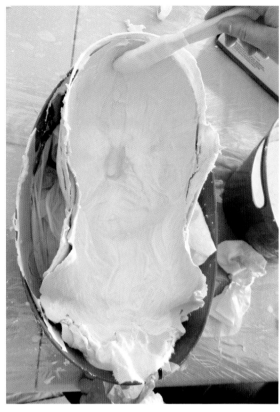
Make sure the splash coat covers all the face in an even layer.

Step 15: Although the plaster cast should come away from the alginate face cast cleanly, it may stick to any other exposed plaster bandage. A thin layer of petroleum jelly or Vaseline will create a barrier and prevent this from happening.

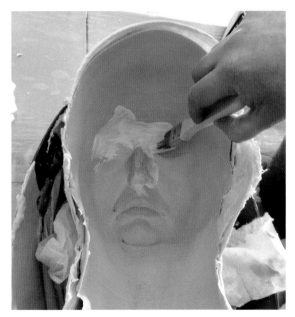
Using a cheap disposable brush, apply a thin detail layer of plaster, known as a splash coat.

Using Vaseline on any exposed edges will prevent the final plaster mould from sticking to the plaster bandage cast.

Step 16: Another way you can reinforce the plaster cast and make it stronger is to use hemp or burlap. This is put into the plaster mix, allowing the plaster to stick to the fabric, and can be used to line the cast, ultimately making it stronger. Make sure to squeeze out the excess plaster using the same technique as for the plaster bandages.

Press burlap into the plaster.

Coat the burlap in plaster.

Squeeze out the excess plaster.

Place plaster-soaked burlap pieces into the face cast to strengthen it.

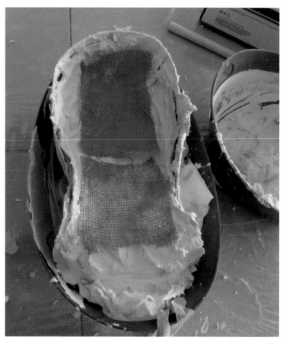

Continue to build up layers of plaster and bandage.

Step 17: After completing the splash or detail coat, add a bit more plaster so that when you put down the plaster-soaked burlap it won't damage the detail layer. Line the edges and inside of the cast with these strips for added strength.

Step 18: By this stage the plaster should have started to cure and will be a more workable consistency. When it is like this you will be able to butter it on using a spatula to make it nice and smooth. Another addition you can add at this point is a handle that will make it easier to lift the cast out of the mould later. In this case a broom handle has been embedded in the plaster and reinforced with more plaster and burlap.

Step 19: Once the cast has been filled it must be left to dry. The plaster will go through a chemical reaction and will get hot. Once it has cooled down it can be removed. It will continue to harden, but when you first release it will still be soft enough

Tools for cleaning the plaster cast.

Use an old knife to clean the cast.

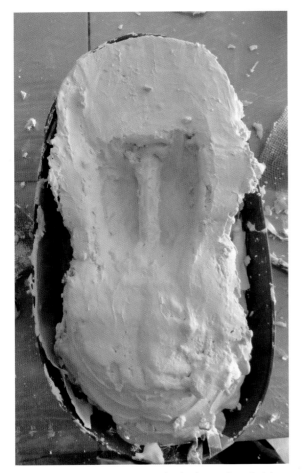

At this point you may want to embed a broom handle into the plaster, which will make it easier to handle the mould.

Carefully press the edge of the knife into the plaster to remove any extra bumps.

for any defects to be tidied up and sharp edges smoothed down. Work carefully, taking off only a little at a time. It's easier to gently remove excess plaster than to put it back if you gouge out too much.

Step 20: The easiest way to open up the nostril area is to use a Dremel multitool. As long as you can see the opening it should be fine. It's beneficial to tidy up the edges of the cast using a rasp, as this will later make moulding easier. If you do tidy the edges, remember to keep all the edges flat and straight. If any of the edges are rounded off this will cause 'undercuts' in the mould, resulting in a situation where the mould locks together, making it impossible to open it without destroying the cast.

At this point you should decide whether you

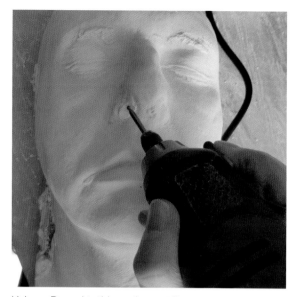

Using a Dremel to tidy up the nostrils.

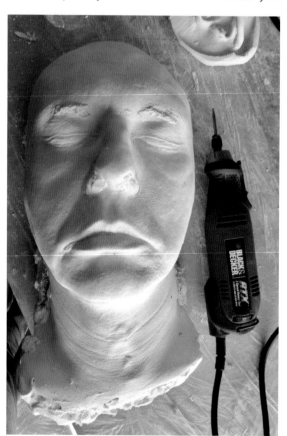

A rotary tool such as a Dremel can be used to take away larger areas, such as the nostrils.

want to make ears for your character (see Chapter 5). If you do, you should make a life cast of the performer's ears while they are still wearing the bald cap.

You may have noticed that the ears were covered by the bald cap when making the face cast. This is because it is easier to cast the ears separately when you are making only a half face cast. Simply cut a hole in the cap and pop the ears out.

It is much more convenient to position the performer on their side when casting ears. This technique will be shown later as a separate project.

As a side note, if you were to cast the performer's entire head you would capture the impression of the ears at the same time. You would then take a separate impression of the ears from the plaster cast head.

For the purpose of this book, however, we shall investigate how to cast and make ears as a standalone project. Let's first look at how to make gelatine, which will be the main material used for the prosthetics in this book. The recipe will make enough for the ear demonstration and the goblin character face.

5

MAKING AND USING GELATINE

In this chapter we are going to look at using gelatine as a prosthetic material. It's a great medium to learn the art of prosthetics as it's a little more forgiving and less expensive than silicone or foam latex. If you can master this material you can make some very realistic prosthetic appliances. It will also help you understand how moulds work, and you can take that knowledge and develop your skills with more advanced materials in the future.

Materials and tools

- Gelatine granules – 300 Bloom from make-up effects suppliers works best
- Sorbitol – can be found online or from make-up effects suppliers
- Glycerine – can be found online, from make-up suppliers or soap-making suppliers
- Microwave oven (or saucepan and heat source)
- Heatproof gloves
- Heatproof protection for your work surface (a place mat or magazine will do)
- Mixing sticks – a small silicone spatula works well
- Small kitchen scales (or measuring cups)
- Ice cube tray
- Coloured powder or liquid make-up (an inexpensive one in your chosen skin tone). An optional way of showing blood vessels or capillaries is to use flocking fibres. These can be found from make-up supply stores.

WHAT IS GELATINE?

Gelatine is a water-soluble protein made from collagen obtained from various animal body parts. It is created from isolating and dehydrating parts of animals, including skin, bones and tissue. It's used in the food industry as a thickener and is basically the stuff from which gummy candies and jellies are made.

Despite that confectionary connection, please bear in mind that currently there is no vegetarian formula on the market. The type we use for prosthetics is usually made from pork, which can also deter some people from using it for religious reasons. It's always best to mention this in advance rather than avoid an embarrassing situation when a curious performer asks about your materials as you are about to apply them. Get into the habit of asking your performer about allergies and any other special needs. Briefly explain the process and materials used. In this way you can help eliminate surprises and they will appreciate the extra care.

Gelatine comes in the form of sheets, granules or powder. The small packets found in most supermarkets will do for quick out-of-kit effects such as burns and boils, but for facial prosthetic appliances the best gelatine you can use is 300 Bloom pork gelatine. Named after Oscar T. Bloom, who developed the test, the strength of gelatine is measured in grams Bloom, with 300 Bloom at the top of the range. It can be bought from Mouldlife in the UK and Frends in the USA, as well as from other online make-up effects suppliers.

Gelatine can be a great choice to utilize when you first start out practising with prosthetics as it's readily available and reasonably inexpensive. The beauty of it is that you can melt it again and reuse it if your first casting attempt fails.

When coloured correctly you can achieve a realistic skin effect that mirrors the translucency of real skin. It is rivalled only by much more expensive silicone.

While gelatine has its advantages, it isn't always the best choice when used in a humid or hot environment. Gelatine is a natural material that will melt using heat. It can also be broken down by water, including tears, saliva and sweat. There are some preventative measures you can take to help counteract this by sealing the pieces (more on this later).

If you are dealing with such conditions you may ultimately find that another material might be a better solution. Another factor is that gelatine can be heavy if the pieces are sculpted too thick. When you design a character you must evaluate your make-up requirements and choose a suitable material. Cost, weight, movement and environment should all be considered.

HOW TO MAKE YOUR OWN PROSTHETIC GELATINE

Before you start, gather together all the supplies mentioned in the materials list.

There are a number of recipes for making prosthetic gelatine that can be used, so it may be worth experimenting to see what works for you. The following example can be adjusted as necessary to suit the amount you need as it can be stored in a fridge for a very long time:

1 part gelatine (100g or 3.5oz)
2.5 parts Sorbitol (250g or 8.8oz)
2.5 parts glycerine (300g or 10.6oz)

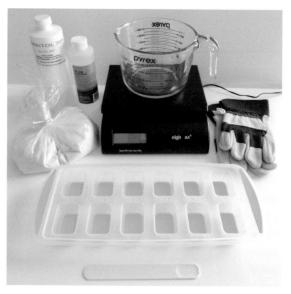

Materials for making prosthetic gelatine.

The mixture must not be lumpy: a smooth and more liquid mixture will yield better pieces. More gelatine granules can always be added to thicken it if necessary.

If you don't have access to a microwave you could mix everything in a bowl placed over a saucepan of hot water, using the same method you would use to melt chocolate.

If you don't have measuring scales, you can always use measuring cups.

The gelatine can be measured out using either scales or measuring cups.

Step 1: Measure out the components into a microwaveable heatproof dish and stir everything together well. It's advisable to leave the mixture for a few hours, preferably overnight, to allow the granules to absorb as much moisture as possible.

Place the mixture in a heatproof jug.

Step 2: Stir the mixture again, then remove the stirrer and place the mixture into the microwave. Adjust the power on the microwave to the lowest setting and set the timer to one or two minutes, repeating as necessary. All microwaves vary, so it is important to keep a close eye on the mixture. Remember to protect the work surface from the heat of the container when you remove it. Using

heatproof gloves, remove the mixture from the microwave, evaluate the consistency and re-stir. The aim is to melt the granules until the mixture is smooth. Please note, it is very easy to burn the mixture and the resulting smell is less than delightful.

Step 3: Always use heatproof gloves when holding the vessel as it will still be extremely hot. When the mixture is thoroughly melted and all the gelatine granules have dissolved, you can add colour to the mixture. In this case tinted powder make-up and a little liquid make-up were used. The colour can be tweaked using blue, green, red and yellow matt eyeshadow powders, although this isn't always necessary. You can also use food colouring. Liquid foundation has the advantage of allowing you to quickly and easily match the skin tone of the performer who will eventually wear the prosthetics.

Whatever colouring method you use, add it sparingly to start with. Gelatine has a natural translucency that mimics skin very well, but you don't want to add so much colour that it turns opaque. If the translucency is right the piece will require little colouring during the application stage and it will be easier to colour realistically.

Use a microwave to melt the mixture for 1 or 2 minutes at a time.

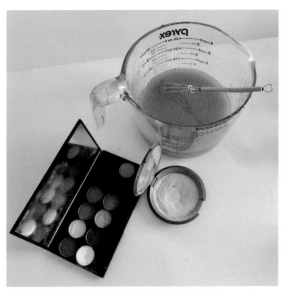

You can use pigments to colour your gelatine.

Remember that a little goes a long way. It's always easier to add more pigment or colour later, but much more difficult to correct an over-coloured batch. If it gets too dark you will have to start all over. One trick is to add uncoloured gelatine to the mix if you find it has gone too opaque.

Another great addition to your colouring technique is flock, finely chopped polyester fibres that come in a variety of colours and add realism to your appliances. The fibres become suspended in the final casting and resemble capillaries. Only a tiny amount on the tip of a mixing stick is needed. It's relatively cheap, but if you are on a budget only a red capillary colour is necessary. Use it to enhance the colour of the mix and not to fully colour the gelatine.

Remember you can also leave the gelatine in its natural state and colour it later when you have decided how you will use it.

Step 4: When you are happy with the colour of the gelatine, pour the mixture into ice cube trays, again using the heatproof gloves, and pop them

Once set the cubes can be stored in a ziplock bag in a fridge for a long time.

into the freezer. In a few hours you will be able to remove the cubes from the mould, put them in a ziplock bag or container and store them in a fridge, although any environment will do as long as it's cool, dark and dry. You now have convenient sized cubes that can be remelted when needed.

This recipe will yield sufficient gelatine for the Goblin make-up and also for making some prosthetic ears.

MAKING GELATINE EARS

In order to make ears that fit the performer exactly you are going to need a life cast of their ears. On this occasion the performer's ears were cast at the same time as his face, so he was already wearing a bald cap to protect his hair from the alginate.

If you are only interested in casting ears you don't need a bald cap. Instead place a large piece of plastic, such as a ziplock bag, on the side of the performer's face, make a small hole and gently pull their ear through the hole. The hole needs to accommodate the ear, yet also be small enough to protect the person's hair. Make sure the actual bag is large enough to cover the rest of the hair. You do not want to discover the hard way that hair and alginate are a bad combination.

Use heatproof gloves when pouring the mixture into the ice cube tray.

Before you start you should set up your area and gather together all the necessary equipment. You should also refer back to the information about life casting in Chapter 4, particularly about the safety measures that should be taken when working with alginate.

Materials and tools

- Cushion
- Waste bin liner
- Large ziplock bags (if you aren't using a bald cap)
- Large plastic cup – this needs to fit over the ear with room around the edges
- Old scissors – to cut the cup
- Small brush
- Mixing container
- Mixing sticks (wooden tongue depressors or similar)
- Alginate
- Cotton wool ball – to block the ear
- Petroleum jelly
- Small rasp
- Small plaster knife or metal clean-up tools
- Water clay (cheap pottery clay will do)
- Sculpting tools
- Kitchen towel
- Water spritzer
- Cooking oil spray
- Silicone moulding material – the silicone casting trial kits made by OOMOO are a good choice for this application, although any type of silicone will work
- Elastic bands – to hold the mould together (you can also use a weight or flat heavy item)
- Pre-made gelatine cubes (see recipe above)
- Alcohol activated inks – to colour the completed ear
- IPA – Isopropyl alcohol (99%)
- Pros-Aide adhesive
- Protection for the work surface – the hot vessel containing the melted gelatine could cause damage, so put down a place mat or something similar.

This is the most basic method of making ears, although it is just one way of doing it and various other techniques may be chosen. Using gelatine for the ears gives them a translucent quality. It is also a good material for practising with when you are starting out as it can be melted again if it doesn't work out the first time. The more you practise with the materials and techniques the better you will become.

Step 1: Put a cushion or pillow into a bin bag and seal it up. Ask the performer to lay their head on the pillow with their face turned to the side. Place a small piece of cotton wool inside the ear to prevent alginate getting into the eardrum. Put a little Vaseline around the ear on any hair that may show as a precautionary measure. If you are casting someone with long hair, tie their hair up tightly out of the way.

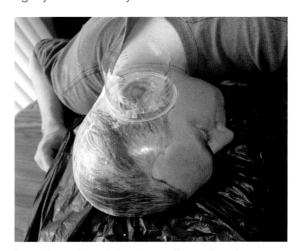

Place the performer's head on a pillow and put the cup around their ear, making sure their head is level.

Step 2: Cut the base off the cup with scissors, making sure that it's deep enough for the alginate to cover the ear once it's poured inside. You will need to help the performer get into the correct position as they need to be level when you pour in the liquid. Place the mouth of the cup over their ear. Keep the ear in the middle with an even amount of space all around it.

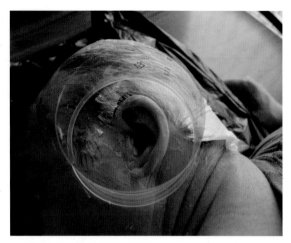

In this view of the position for casting an ear, note how the bottom of the cup has been cut away.

Step 3: Mix the alginate according to the manufacturer's instructions. Make sure you have first carried out a test to check the setting time and adjusted the temperature of the water accordingly. Since this is a fast cast technique, you can make the water a little warmer, which will accelerate the alginate's curing time.

Using your fingers, start by putting some alginate behind the ear, making sure you don't trap any air bubbles. You can then use a small brush or your fingers to push the alginate around the details of the ears before pouring in the rest of

the mix. This will ensure you capture all the intricate details of the ear. As the alginate is flexible once cured, don't worry about it getting into the folds of the ears. You need it to capture everything and it will all come off cleanly.

Step 4: Once the alginate has set you can remove the cast. The plastic cup will support it, enabling it to hold its shape. Gently wiggle it around and it will be released from the ear. The cotton ball you placed inside the ear canal usually comes out with the alginate cast. Since alginate can shrink, you should pour the plaster into the alginate mould as soon as possible.

Begin filling the mould with a small amount of the mixed plaster. Tap on the side of the alginate mould to help release the air bubbles to the top of the cast and gently blow on them to pop them. Once the plaster has cured and cooled you can carefully remove it from the alginate mould. Be extremely careful as the ear will be delicate and you don't want to break it. You should then clean up any sharp edges with a rasp.

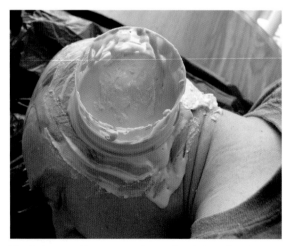

Block the ear with cotton and pour the alginate into the cup.

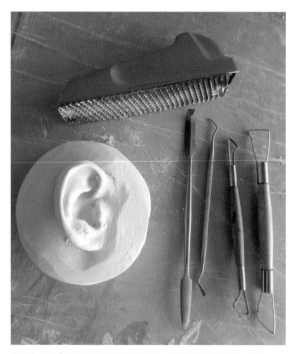

Any imperfections should be cleaned up with tools like these.

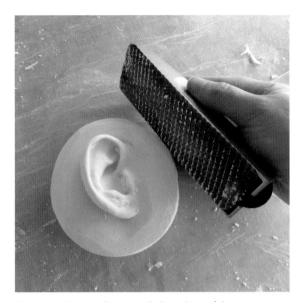

A rasp can be used to smooth the edges of the cast.

Step 5: Now you have exact replicas of the performer's ears you are ready to sculpt your new ears. This time water-based clay has been used as it is quick to work with and can easily be cleaned out of the ear and the mould. For this demo we are making an oversized cartoonish ear, although depending on the look you are going for, you could make just an ear tip if you wish. Study the contours of the ear cast, following the lines of the ear as you will want the piece to blend seamlessly to the real ear. When sculpting the new ear you can exaggerate the character's features to make them more interesting.

Back ear view. Note where the clay ear ends on the plaster ear cast.

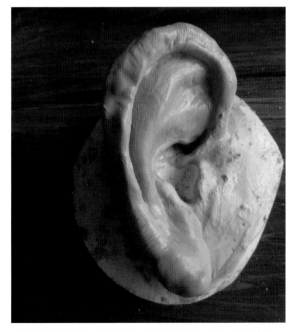

This is the new clay ear that has been sculpted onto the plaster ear cast.

A comparison of the new ear with the original ear cast. These are cartoon ears and are much bigger than the original.

Second ear sculpt roughed out in clay.

Step 6: One of the advantages of having the ears cast as two separate components is that you can place them side by side to make sure they match up when you start to sculpt the second ear. They don't need to be identical, in fact they should be a little different, but at least the proportions can be matched up.

Step 7: When you come to cast the ear you will need to build out a platform around the

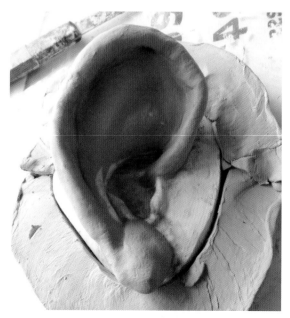

Starting to build out the platform around the ear to make a mould for the silicone pour.

ear sculpt. Water-based clay can be used for this.

You will also need to create a cutting edge around the edge of the sculpt. This will create the blending edge on the prosthetic ear. Next you need to build a wall around the ear so you can pour the silicone over the entire ear sculpt to create the negative mould.

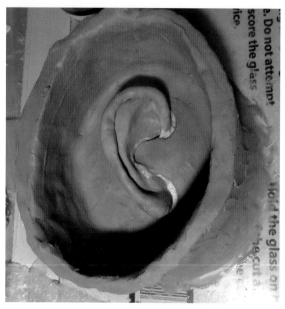

A wall should be built around the ear to hold the silicone that will eventually become the ear mould.

Step 8: While you are prepping the second ear, you can help keep the clay on the ear from drying out by wrapping it in moistened paper towel. If you need to leave it overnight, wrap a plastic carrier bag around it as well. This will keep it preserved until you are ready to mould it.

When it comes to moulding, simply mix up a two-part silicone A and B component, using the high pour technique (as described in Chapter 3) to eliminate any air bubbles. Any two-part silicone product can be used. In this case PlatSil Gel 25 from Mouldlife was chosen, but another good option would be OOMOO by Smooth-on, which has a 1:1 ratio mix, so you don't need scales or a degasser to get rid of air bubbles.

Cover the clay sculpt with damp kitchen roll paper to stop the clay drying out.

Step 9: When the silicone is cured, remove the two parts and clean the clay off thoroughly. The next stage involves filling the ear mould with gelatine (refer back to earlier in this chapter for more advice). Cooking spray can be used as a release spray. This is cheap and widely available in supermarkets. You could also use Vaseline, but the cooking spray works well and it gets into all the ear's crevices. Be careful not to let it pool in the mould, removing any excess with a paper towel.

Spray the inside of the mould with cooking spray as a release agent.

Only use the spray in the silicone mould, as this will encourage the new gelatine ear to remain attached to the ear cast.

Step 10: Next you need to melt the gelatine (once again referring back to the safety precautions outlined above). Use a suitable microwave-safe container and heatproof gloves when handling the hot container. You should also remember to protect the work surface. If you wish you can

Melt the pre-made gelatine and pour it into the silicone mould.

warm up the receiving negative/recessed mould to help the gelatine flow more easily, but it's not necessary for such a small mould. Make sure you don't create air bubbles in the mould (popping them if you see them) and that the gelatine has flowed all around the mould. Fill it close to the top. It doesn't matter if there is a little overflow when the two parts of the mould are placed together as this indicates there is enough material in the mould.

Step 11: When you put both moulds together, keep the negative mould into which you poured the gelatine on the bottom. Allow the ear cast

Set your plaster ear into the gelatine until it comes out over the edges a little, and secure it with elastic bands.

alcohol-activated inks. If you study ears you will notice they are a lot redder than the rest of the face. Copy this colouring when painting the prosthetic ear. Finally check it against the performer's ear to see how it looks. Pros-Aide or Telesis 5 can be used to glue the ear when you are ready.

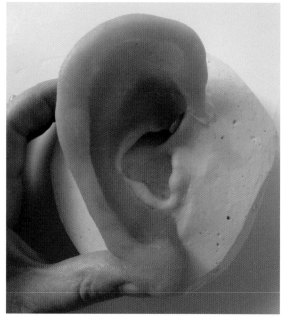

Here is the final gelatine when it has set and been removed from the mould.

to find its position in the other mould and press firmly on the top. Maintain this pressure for a few minutes, then carefully attach some elastic bands, making sure not to dislodge the fit of the ear cast in the mould, and then place the entire mould in the freezer for about 60 minutes or longer, depending on the thickness of the design. After this time it should have set fully. If you keep a little material in the heatproof jug you will be able to check when it has cured. This will let you gauge when the freezer mould is ready.

Step 12: Carefully remove the two moulds. You may find that a little baby powder will help to release the ear. The greasy release you sprayed into the mould should be carefully cleaned off with some IPA.

Once this is complete you are ready to paint and apply the ear. You will need to seal the back and front of the piece with a sealer such as Kryolan Fixing Spray, which is sprayed into a container so you can paint it on. Do not paint right up to the edge, but leave a 0.5cm gap as this will be your blending edge. You can also use Pros-Aide liquid as a sealer, but you must powder it well as it sticks to itself.

Once the piece is sealed it can be painted with

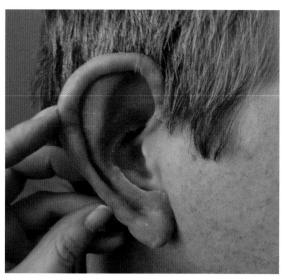

You can now paint your ear and offer it up to the performer to check the fit before gluing it in place.

6

SCULPTING, MOULDING AND CASTING A ONE-PIECE APPLIANCE

Now that you have a replica of the performer's face you are ready to sculpt an appliance that will be an exact custom fit. This will allow optimum movement as the piece will line up exactly with all the muscles in the face. Technically a generic prosthetic appliance can be made to fit most people. It usually takes some skill to work with a generic prosthetic as you will have to tweak pieces like this to help them fit better, but a custom-made piece is a joy to work with as everything locks perfectly into position.

Materials and tools

- Life cast of your performer (see Chapter 4 for details)
- Rust-Oleum Crystal Clear gloss lacquer spray paint
- Monster Clay or other oil-based non-drying clay medium
- Selection of sculpting tools
- Chip brush – uncut
- Naphtha or lighter fluid
- Mini gas blowtorch – a small kitchen one is ideal
- Isopropyl alcohol (IPA)
- Baby powder
- Selection of cleaning brushes – usually one of each in metal, plastic

and brass (cheap examples may be found in hardware or bargain stores)
- Reference pictures – gather as many pictures of real people as you need. It is always best to work from life rather than attempting to copy other people's work, as you will get more realistic results.

In order to help the clay stick to the life cast and also to seal it, which will help later when it comes to casting the negative mould, two thin layers of clear gloss spray are first added to the cast.

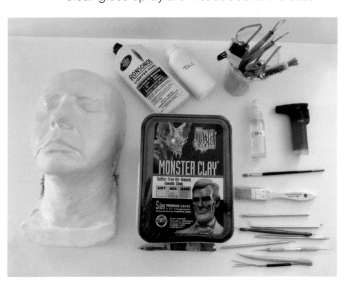

Sculpting materials.

CHOOSE THE SCULPTING MEDIUM

There are many options available when it comes to sculpting. The two main types of clay are water-based and oil-based. Water-based clay is mostly used for building walls around sculpts, but some artists also like to sculpt with it. It can produce fast results as it is soft and pliable and large forms can be made quickly, but it also runs the risk of drying out, which can make it a little difficult to sculpt wispy details.

WED clay made by Laguna is very popular among FX artists and mask makers. WED was developed for animatronic models made by the Disney studio (and took its name from Walter E. Disney). Also known as EM-217, WED has become quite popular in the film industry for creating large detailed sculptures. The addition of glycerine in the mix means that it dries more slowly than traditional water-based clay.

Oil-based clay has the advantage of never drying out, so you can simply walk away from a sculpt without having to mist it with water and cover it up, and it will be good as new when you return. You should always look for a sulphur-free oil-based clay, as it is a better choice when it comes to making silicone moulds. The sulphur can sometimes inhibit the silicone's curing, so it's safer to avoid it.

Chavant produces a good range of clays in different hardnesses, but for this sculpt we will use Monster Clay, which is a simply amazing sculpting medium. It's reasonably priced and you get a lot of it. It doesn't dry out and has a great texture when worked. Monster Clay's sulphur-free, low-melt formulation can be reused over and over as it always returns to its original firm state on cooling, which is definitely a bonus when you are starting out. It's easily softened with heat, enabling large forms to be built up rapidly with minimal effort.

Monster Clay comes in a convenient container that can withstand heating up to 93°C (200°F) and allows the clay to be carefully heated to make it pliable and, if necessary, pourable. Some people like to use a double boiler or an old slow electric cooker or crock pot to heat it and keep it warm.

SCULPTING THE FACE

Step 1: Since this demo is for beginners and we want to limit the need for expensive equipment, we will use the technique of heating it carefully with a heat gun or gas torch to soften the top layer and then scrape it off with a sculpting tool into ribbons of clay.

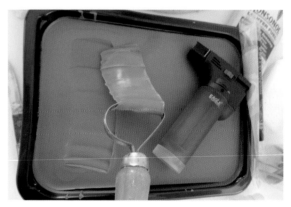

Softening the clay.

Step 2: Start by using the clay ribbons to compose the rough forms. Keep this layer thin to begin with, since thinner pieces will enable more movement. A useful tip is to mark the point of a sharp sculpting tool with the desired measurement of thickness. That way you can insert it into the clay and determine the depth. You can test thin areas too, but you don't want part of the sculpt to get too thin or the finished piece might tear. When laying clay around the openings of the mouth and eyes you need to keep it thin so that the edges blend seamlessly into the skin. Be mindful of the angles too. Everything needs to be subtle, so make sure the transition between the plaster cast and the new sculpt is gradual. Leave enough room around the eyes: you don't want

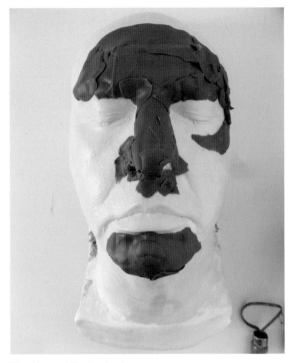

Blocking out the basic shape.

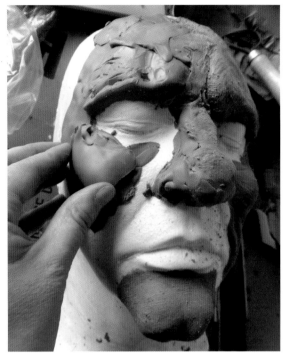

Building up the rough shape.

the finished piece to be so heavy on top of the performer's eyelid that it forces the eye closed.

Step 3: Start to add more depth to the areas of the face you want to build up in order to help add character. This make-up is going to illustrate how someone's appearance can really be transformed, so the nose, chin and forehead are going to be changed dramatically. It's also a mythical character, so the proportions are going to be exaggerated to increase the whimsical appearance. Even if your character isn't based in reality, studying human and animal anatomy will help make your sculpting more realistic.

Step 4: When you are happy with the basic shape of the face sculpt, you need to smooth out the clay using raking tools. A cheap sculpting tool can be turned into an excellent rake by wrapping fine jewellery wire around the tip, as shown here. You will be able to work quite quickly with such a tool.

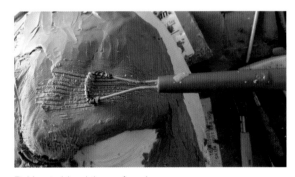

Raking to blend the surface layer.

Step 5: When you are raking out the rough texture of your sculpt you should get used to working with the contours of the face. The marks made by the rake in the photograph overleaf illustrate the direction in which the rake should be used. This is going to be a one-piece facial appliance, almost like a mask, with the thinnest areas around the top lip and mouth. Here they have been left for now so you can see how thin the sculpt is in this area.

Basic shape.

Step 6: You can now start to mark out some of the details on the sculpt, which will help you see where the final design is headed.

It's very easy to get carried away with putting in fine details and textures at this point, so try to get everything roughed out first. Don't worry

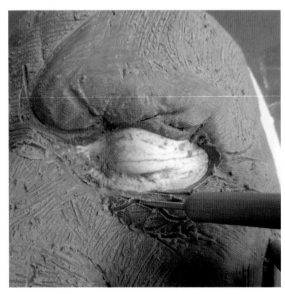

Marking out the details.

if you need to make changes as your sculpt will constantly change and evolve until you are happy.

Step 7: When sculpting skin textures an invaluable tool comes as part of a cheap wire brush set intended for cleaning welding slag and rust. These usually come in a pack of three (plastic, steel and brass) and they work extremely well on this type of clay, mimicking the texture of skin. Don't be scared to run them over the clay in different directions as you can be quite firm. Also don't worry about the little clay balls that come away when using these tools, since you can get rid of them later using talc.

Using a cross-hatching technique will quickly build a realistic texture. You should try to make the texture on the sculpt match the texture on the life cast.

Step 8: The best way to create the appearance of deep wrinkles is to make some clay sausages and place them over the areas where they are wanted.

Step 9: Next use another rake to blend the edges of the wrinkles into the rest of the face, following this with the wire brush tool to smooth it out further. These techniques can also be used for wrinkles around the eyes.

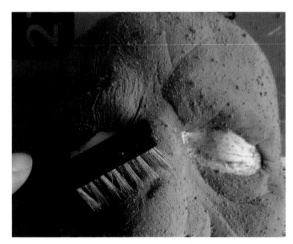

Smoothing the surface.

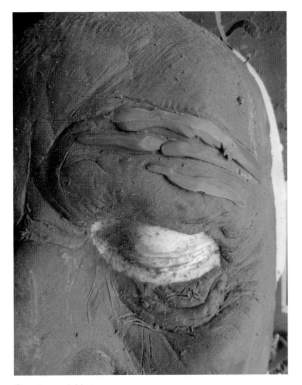

Creating wrinkles.

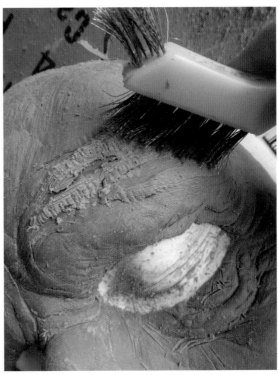

Brushing the wrinkles.

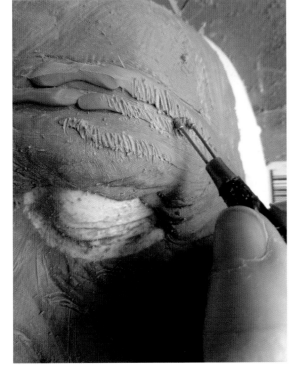

Blending the wrinkles.

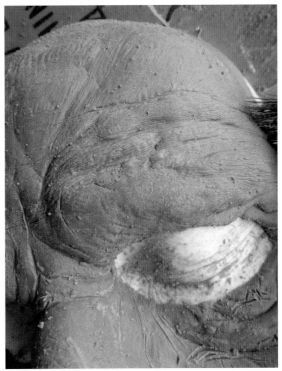

The completed wrinkles.

View of the wrinkles from above.

Step 10: Keep on using the metal brush to get rid of tool marks over the face. You will notice that using this brush gathers lots of little balls of clay on the face. The best technique to get rid of these is to dust the face with talc and a chip brush.

Step 11: You are now starting to get into the finer details of the sculpt. Another technique for adding skin texture is to place a plastic bag over the sculpt and rake over the plastic. This eliminates the balls of clay and allows a more

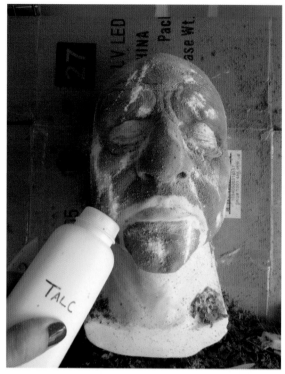

Talc and clay balls.

More smoothing can create small clay balls.

Removing the clay balls.

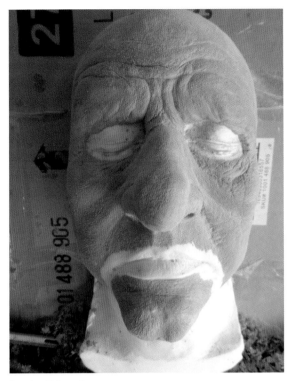

Brush off the talc.

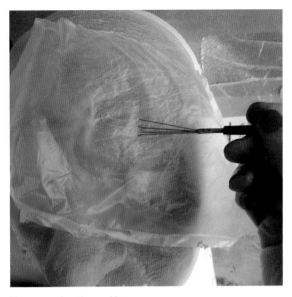

Home-made rake and bag.

an aluminium tube. The wire can be sealed by pinching the ends of the tube together, although for added security you could seal the wire with strong epoxy putty or car body filler.

rounded recess on the wrinkle. The best type of plastic for this is the plastic bubble pouches used for mail packages. You can experiment with other thicknesses of plastic: sandwich bags and ziplock bags will also give interesting textures.

Another useful tool is a home-made rake created by inserting piano wire into the end of

Step 12: You can add deeper texture and lines using a rounded tool, blending them in with the plastic brush, which is softer than the metal one.

Raking over a plastic bag can add skin texture.

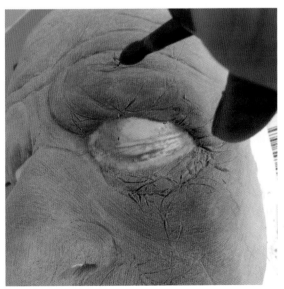

Finer detail can now be introduced.

As your sculpt evolves, look around to see where else you can add texture or more wrinkles. It's important to take the occasional break and come back to the work with fresh eyes. Keep referring back to your reference. Try to keep working on both sides at the same time. It's very easy to concentrate on one side, but you need to make sure everything is balanced.

Adding more wrinkles.

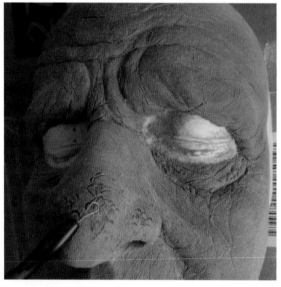

Still more skin texture.

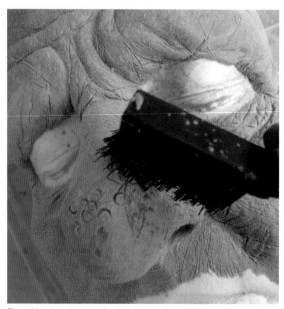

Blending in with a soft plastic brush.

Make sure the two sides are balanced.

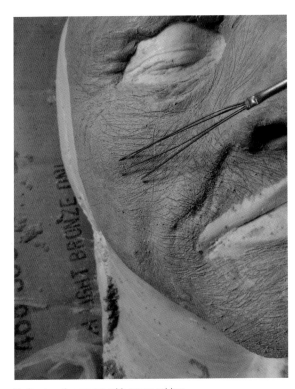

Softening the pores with more raking.

Step 13: When you are happy with the overall result, for a final touch you can add some texture to the pores on the face, softening some of them with the rake and a little lighter fluid on a brush. It will be helpful if you study the patterns made by pores on a real face or life cast.

Step 14: After you have powdered the sculpt, you can give it a spritz with IPA and buff it in gently with a full-length chip brush to give a final polish. You are now ready to mould the sculpt.

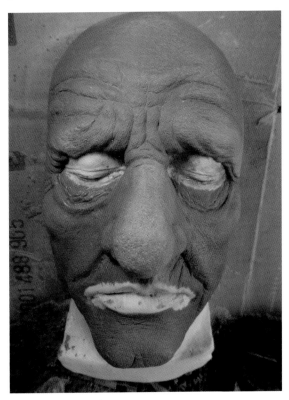

The completed sculpt.

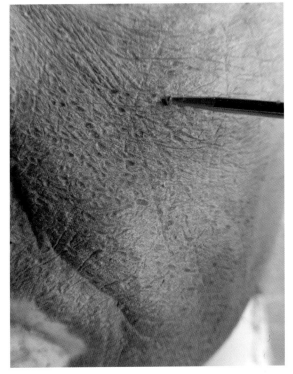

Pore texture.

TOP TIP

Remember that the more experience you have applying make-up the better you will become at sculpting facial forms. You will quickly learn what works on a face and what doesn't.

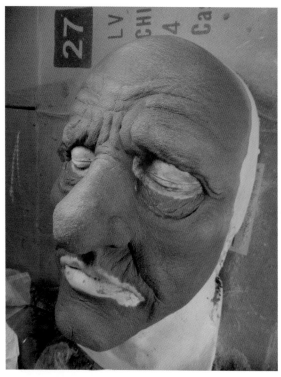

Further angles show more detail.

MOULDING AND CASTING THE APPLIANCE

The sculpt we have is in one piece. In order to make a prosthetic appliance from it we need to turn this into a one-piece mould. Moulding can be a tricky concept for those new to it, so this section of the book breaks it down into simple-to-follow diagrams. You will see how to make a one-piece mould of the character sculpted earlier on. This is a relatively simple mould that can be made quickly and is good for beginners.

Materials and tools

- PlatSil Gel 25 silicone A and B
- TinThix liquid thickening agent
- Silicone pigment (choice of any two different colours)
- Ultra 4 epoxy parfilm (release spray)
- Large mixing cups
- Plaster bandage or Hydrocal plaster and burlap
- Scales
- Small ice cube tray
- Disposable chip brushes 3–4
- Vinyl gloves (not latex)
- Mixing sticks
- Sharpie (permanent marker)
- Scissors
- Oil-based clay (e.g. Monster Clay)
- Sculpting tool
- Vaseline
- Hairdryer
- Fixer spray (e.g. Kryolan Fixing Spray, Ben Nye Final Seal or Green Marble SeLr)
- Talc
- Powder brush
- IPA
- The finished sculpt
- Gelatine
- Microwave
- Microwave-proof jug
- Heatproof gloves
- Heat protection for work surface (placemat or magazine)

Undercuts

Undercuts are areas in the mould that have potential to lock together, causing disastrous results that may even mean you will never get the mould apart without damage. An undercut is basically anywhere that hooks around or has a ledge. Areas such as the sides of the nostril, under the nose and under the chin are all potential areas for undercuts.

When this particular mould is complete it will have to be removed by pulling on the top of the forehead in a forward and down motion. The angles of the nose and chin would make it difficult if we tried to release the mould from the chin upwards. If you are having difficulty working out where undercuts might be, a tip is to stand directly over the sculpt and look down at it: the areas you can't see are where the undercuts

Undercuts should always be avoided.

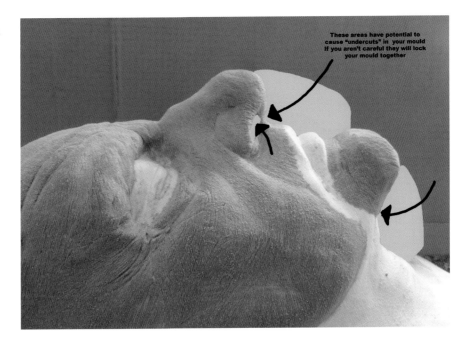

are lurking. If you attempted a one-piece mould of this character in plaster alone you might get lucky, but it is likely you would have a tough time getting it apart. This is the reason why we are using silicone to create the detail layer of the face and then using a plaster jacket to support the flexible silicone. It's less risky for a one-piece mould.

Creating a cutting edge

Another important step in creating a prosthetic appliance is the cutting edge, the fine feathered edge that will allow you to blend the prosthetic seamlessly into the performer's skin. In order to do this you need to build small angled walls or plates around all the areas where the cutting edge needs to be.

In this particular sculpt the edges will be around the eyes, mouth and all around the edge of the face. All these areas need to have a cutting edge sculpted on them. To make this easier to follow, a different coloured clay has been used to illustrate this, and for this a softer oil-based clay works best.

Step 1: Fill the centre of each area, leaving a gap of about 0.5cm where you can still see the plaster life cast. The height of each piece should be about 0.5–1cm. The most important thing to remember is that the outer rim of each of these

Creating cutting edges.

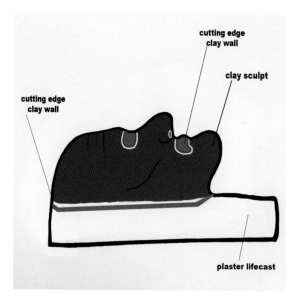

Cutting edge diagram.

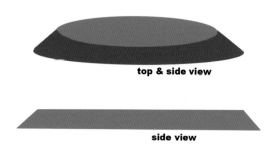

Edge angles.

green sculpted areas needs to be completely smooth. You then need to take a fine-edged sculpting tool or small craft knife and, holding it at a slight angle, go around the outside edge of each of these green areas. The one right round the jawline only requires an angle on the edge next to the life cast. Be extra careful that you don't scrape the plaster life cast when doing this.

Step 2: When you have completed sculpting the cutting edges, run a thin layer of Vaseline along the areas where the life cast is exposed. The silicone shouldn't really stick to it, but it's better to be safe than sorry. At this stage give the entire cast a spray with a release agent, such as Ultra 4 epoxy parfilm.

Step 3: Gather together all the materials and tools listed for working the silicone equipment. For this mould we will be using PlatSil Gel 25. As it has a 1:1 mix ratio scales will not be essential, but the advantage of using scales is that they give more accuracy and you only need to use one mixing cup, since everything can be mixed in the same vessel.

Depending on the size and shape of the sculpt you need to work out how much product you will need. Start with a total of about 400g (200g of each component) and see how you go. You may need more or less, but this is a good start.

PlatSil Gel 25 has a fast set time with a pot life of only 5 minutes, which is the time from the moment the two components touch each other. You need to mix it quickly and get it on to your mould accurately and quickly.

Because this is a platinum-based silicone you must use only vinyl gloves with it, since latex can inhibit the cure.

You should also remember to label the necessary equipment 'A' and 'B' to avoid cross-contamination.

Step 4: The first thing you should do is make some keys. You can buy specially designed trays for this, but small ice cube trays work well too, although you might need to cut them in half with scissors if they are too big once cured.

Give the ice cube tray a generous spray of Ultra 4 epoxy parfilm spray release, mix up a small batch of PlatSil Gel 25, fill the ice cube tray and set this aside to cure. To be doubly safe, you could make them in advance the night before.

Step 5: For the first silicone layer we are going to use a mix of PlatSil Gel 25 A and B with a little silicone pigment in it. The colour isn't important, but this helps to show you how well you've covered everything and is particularly helpful when it comes to adding a second layer. The first layer is brushed on using a disposable chip brush, which should not be cut down as it has to be full and soft. Mix up the first batch and pour

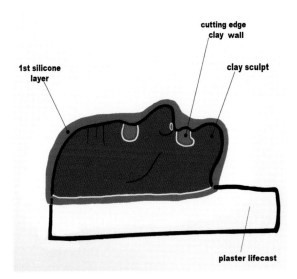

First silicone layer.

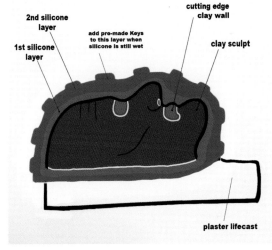

Second silicone layer and keys.

it gently over the sculpt, letting it drizzle over the entire form and very gently using the brush to move it around as necessary. You have about 5 minutes from when you start until it begins to feel tacky. Stop at once or you will risk pulling up the fine layer you have put down. The purpose of this first layer is to capture the detail. This is known as the detail coat.

Step 6: Make sure the pre-made keys are ready for use. Mix up another batch of PlatSil Gel 25 and then add a different coloured pigment to it. This time you are going to add some TinThix, which is an interference medium that does what it says on the tin, thickening the silicone to a brushable consistency. You need only two or three drops as this stuff is potent. Just mix it up and you will see it thicken. Often you will find that adding thickener to the silicone retards the cure and stretches your worktime slightly.

Since the detail coat is already completed, you can now butter this on top, though you still need to be gentle so as not to damage the sculpt. Use another chip brush as the first will now have cured silicone on it. The reason for making this layer a different colour is to make sure that you get an even coat that covers the first coloured layer.

The surface of this layer needs to be as smooth as possible and you can use a wooden tongue depressor to smooth out any bumps. While this layer is still wet, position the keys at intervals around the edges of the sculpt. You can also put a couple on the top if you wish. These will help to lock the plaster jacket into the silicone better and enable the plaster to lock into place more easily when dried.

The silicone will take about an hour to cure, when it can then be taken out of the mould. Again keep a little in the mixing pot so you can check if it has set. While you are waiting for it to set you can get on with the next step.

Step 7: You now need to create a hard shell that will cover the silicone layer, much like the technique used when making the life cast. For this you can use Hydrocal plaster and burlap or plaster bandages, though the Hydrocal will be substantially stronger.

Let the plaster thicken a little and brush a layer all over the mould, making sure to work it all around the keys. Dip the burlap in the plaster and shape it over this initial layer, building up more plaster as you go along.

Mix up the plaster with warmer water as you

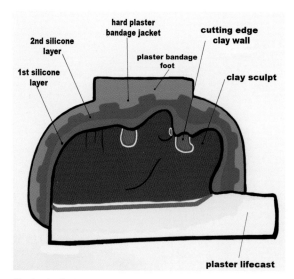

Plaster jacket.

want to speed up the set time. You need to cover all the areas on which you just put the silicone. Make an additional foot on the very top of the mould to give it a steady surface to stand on when you flip it over. This can be done by twisting ropes of burlap into a circle.

Leave the mould to fully cure overnight.

Step 8: When it comes to removing the new mould you've just made, this must be done extremely carefully. Leaving the mould in the same position as you made it, stand in front and try to pull the plaster jacket carefully from the top of the forehead towards your body. It should come off easily, but if not you might need to flip the entire mould over onto the foot that you made for it. Using the handle you made on the face cast, you can pull to try to separate the two moulds. If this doesn't work you might need to lever it apart by attempting to insert two long-handled screwdrivers, or something similar, into the silicone on either side and levering it up.

Step 9: When you manage to get the moulds apart you need to clean away every trace of the clay. Do this carefully with a wooden or plastic tool, since metal can risk damaging the mould.

Step 10: When both moulds are cleaned you need to put some release on them before adding the gelatine. You could use cooking spray, as with the ears (see Chapter 5), or simply Vaseline with an added layer of Ultra 4. Remember if you choose to use Vaseline and brush it on, heat it up a little so that it spreads more easily.

You are now ready to fill the mould with the pre-made gelatine (for more details on melting it, see Chapter 5). Put it in the microwave and heat for periods of a minute at a time until it is ready. You should check it regularly because it burns easily and burnt gelatine has the most vile smell. Use a heatproof jug and heatproof gloves.

Once melted to a liquid consistency you are ready to pour it into the mould. Make sure it's standing on its foot so that the mould resembles a bowl, then pour in the mix, swirling it around to make sure everything is covered. You may need more gelatine than you think as you have to allow for a little overflow. This will indicate you have adequately filled the mould when you apply pressure. Be careful not to overdo it, however, or you might put the integrity of the edges at risk.

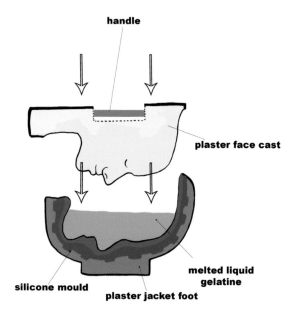

You may need more gelatine than you think.

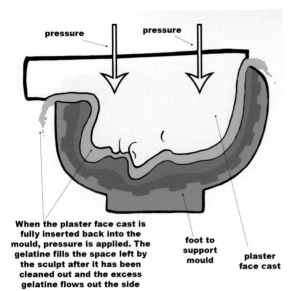

pressure   pressure

When the plaster face cast is fully inserted back into the mould, pressure is applied. The gelatine fills the space left by the sculpt after it has been cleaned out and the excess gelatine flows out the side

foot to support mould

plaster face cast

The completed mould.

Use the handle on the back of the life cast to lower it gently and securely into the mould. You will need to apply pressure to the mould to get good edges, so either strap it up or set something heavy on top. Leave it to set.

The final cast from the mould is an exact replica of the sculpted character. It now needs to be cleaned thoroughly, but carefully, to remove all traces of the mould release. As it is made of gelatine you can use a little IPA on a soft brush or cotton pad. Keep the cast piece stored on the life cast and in a cool environment away from heat sources or direct sunlight until you are ready to paint it and bring this character to life.

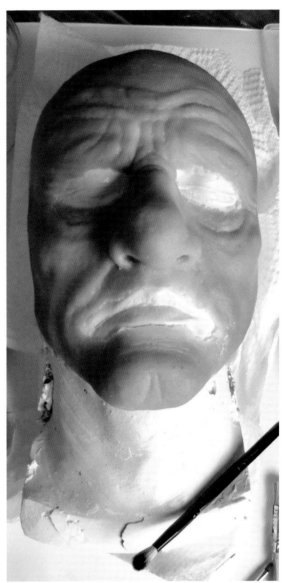

The final cast.

7
ADDING REALISTIC SKIN TONES AND HAIR WORK

The painting technique described in this chapter works best with either gelatine or silicone appliances that have already been cast using the lightest shade of the performer's skin tone.

Materials and tools

- Pros-Aide liquid – the appliance will need to be sealed before painting in order for the paint to stay on
- Make-up sealer – Kryolan Fixing Spray and Ben Nye Final Seal can be used to seal the back of the appliances
- Alcohol-based inks, either dry or liquid (the palette version has been used in this demo)
- Selection of artist's or make-up brushes (see below for details)
- Small chip brush and scissors to cut bristles
- Isopropyl alcohol (IPA) – must be 99 per cent (nothing less will work)
- Cup to hold the IPA
- Small spritzer bottle to hold the IPA (optional)
- Kitchen paper (2 sheets)

Painting realistic skin can be quite challenging. You are trying to fool an audience into believing that your character is real, so you don't want to break that illusion. It has been stated by many professional make-up artists that 'a great paint job is the saving grace of many an appliance'. Painting appliances is an important skill for a

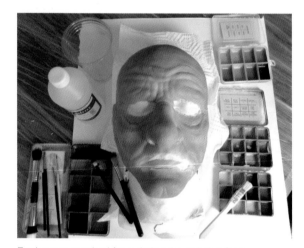
Equipment required for painting the gelatine face.

prosthetic make-up artist. Paint can camouflage the edges and help them melt seamlessly into the performer's real skin.

You will need to study the performer's skin carefully, looking at the undertones of the skin and seeing if there are any freckles or moles. Think about how you can link their natural skin to the prosthetic piece.

Study reference pictures and get used to working with all ethnicities. Observe how skin ages and how it is affected by the environment and people's lifestyle. Always work from real reference photos; don't try to copy another artist's work, as this will make your own work look more authentic.

GETTING STARTED

When it comes to painting silicone or, in this case, gelatine appliances, much of the work has been done for you. Both of these materials, when coloured correctly, have a beautiful translucent quality to them and in their unpainted state already look quite like skin, provided they have been pre-tinted prior to casting.

It is important to follow this theme of translucency when it comes to adding more colour to your appliance. In this demo we will be painting in a technique similar to that of a watercolour artist, using washes of colour to build depth to the skin by suggesting veins and capillaries underneath the epidermis layer, as well as age spots and sun damage on top.

Watercolour artists rarely use white paint on their work – rather the lightest shade is the colour of the paper. We will adopt the same method: the unpainted surface of the appliance will be the lightest colour on the face, with the other colour added in darker shades.

The best medium for use on gelatine prosthetics is an alcohol-activated ink that comes in both a liquid form, which can be airbrushed, and a dry version that comes in set pans. It is highly pigmented and is activated and thinned using 99 per cent alcohol, also known as isopropyl alcohol or IPA. The IPA is used like water when painting with these inks. The colour can be diluted to a very faint translucent wash, or allowing more pigment to mix with the IPA will result in a more opaque finish.

This medium has the advantage of being waterproof. The dry alcohol colours come in a convenient pre-filled plastic palette, which makes them more portable for work on set. They have been categorized into themed colour charts for your convenience. It can be quite overwhelming when you are first starting out as there are so many to choose from. They are essential for any budding professional make-up artist, but they are expensive, so a few tips may help to guide how you use them.

Some of the brands commonly available online, direct from the supplier, or from professional make-up stores are listed below. This is only a sample of what may be available in your area. They are listed in no particular order, but bear in mind that they vary in price so you will have to see what fits your budget. It's useful to note that some brands offer smaller palettes, which can be more economical:

PPI (Premiere Products, Inc) Skin Illustrator
Reel Body Art Ink
Bluebird Inks
W.M. Creations Stacolor
Encore

TOP TIP

When you are starting out, look for palettes that have similar colours to these:

Red, Yellow and Blue (primary colours). You can make any colour from these three, and by adding black and white you can make almost any tone.
Black and White
Olive Green
Blue Vein
Yellow Ochre
Burnt Sienna
Dark Brown
Blood Red

If you purchase a light flesh and a dark flesh palette, you will be able to mix up most skin tones. You should also look for a palette that has the primary colours, as well as black and white. Some blood and dirt colours will also be useful when you have to add casualty effects or grime to your character.

BRUSHES

The ink is applied using a range of brushes. Crownbrush, which is available online in the UK and USA, has a great range of affordable, high-quality brushes available in both animal hair and synthetic. You can also use artists' brushes. You don't need many brushes when starting out and you will quickly find you have favourites that you use all the time. Look after them well and they will last a lifetime. Clean them with IPA and there are all sorts of artists' brush soaps that help preserve the bristles after using the IPA.

For this particular paint job the following brushes were used:

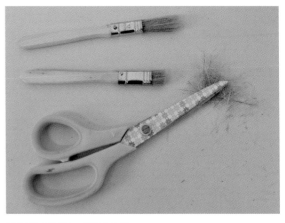

How to create a chip brush.

- Small fine tipped brush – for detail work, such as broken capillaries
- Medium fine tipped brush – for creating shadows in facial wrinkles and lines
- Medium fluffy – to blend the washes of colour
- Fluffy foundation – to stipple washes of colour over large areas
- Disposable chip brush (cut down) – to spatter the paint and give an airbrushed affect

One tool that is invaluable in painting prosthetics is the humble chip brush. Take a cheap brush and trim the bristles down so you are left with a splatter brush. You could also use a toothbrush,

but a chip brush gives superior control over the paint. You must keep your paint translucent but not too drippy. Always practise the spatter on the back of your hand before you commit to applying it to your prosthetic. Alcohol inks are tricky to correct once you start layering them: if you try to remove colour you will leave holes in the paint job. If you need to soften a mistake, use very little IPA on a fine soft brush, delicately touching only the area you wish to lift.

PRE-PAINTING THE CHARACTER STEP BY STEP

Since this is a simple one-piece prosthetic, it will be useful to pre-paint it prior to application, saving time and making the process quicker and more comfortable for the actor. Most prosthetic artists will do some pre-painting for this reason. Usually a performer will play a character over a period of days, weeks or even months, and this almost always means a new prosthetic appliance every day. Often the prosthetic artist will take the unpainted pieces, line them up in rows and pre-paint them all at once, repeating each step on every face. This allows the artist to duplicate almost exactly the paint scheme to maintain the continuity on each appliance. Since continuity

Trimming the bristles of a chip brush.

plays a huge part in the role of an effects artist, it is very important that a master copy of the finished character is produced to use as a template. This will be a fully painted and haired prosthetic that has been mounted onto a face form, usually a plastic duplicate of the actor's life cast.

You may find yourself in a situation where you are given another prosthetic artist's character to apply if they are unable to do it. You will have to apply that make-up on the performer, making sure it looks the same as when the original artist did it.

That's why a master copy is so important. It's there as your guide, accompanied by notes and clear photos. You should get into the habit of photographing your work and any changes or progressions that happen to your character. This is called 'keeping continuity'.

Step 1: The first thing you need to do is to carefully clean any traces of mould release from the prosthetic. Since this piece is made from gelatine it will break down with liquid. Wipe it carefully with a soft brush, clean cotton pad or tissue and some IPA. Don't keep rubbing over the same

areas or you will alter the pore texture that you spent all that time sculpting.

You should also seal the piece at this point. There are a number of ways of doing this. A sealer spray such as Kryolan Fixing Spray is a popular choice. Spray a little into a medicine cup or the lid of the bottle and simply paint it onto your appliance. If you don't have access to this, you could also use a fine layer of Pros-Aide adhesive applied with a very fine-pored sponge and then powder it well with a no-colour translucent powder. This is the technique used on this appliance. Don't paint the sealer right up to the edge. Leave a 0.5cm line to serve as the blending edge.

Don't be tempted to get the hairdryer out to speed up the drying process as you will melt the gelatine appliance. Let everything dry naturally.

Step 2: You are now ready to paint. Load the chip brush with a translucent wash of pinky/red. As the bristles are pulled back the paint is released,

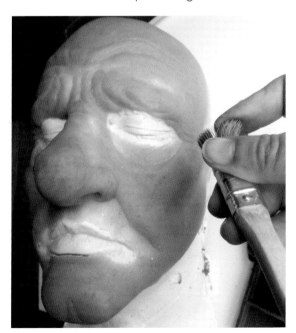

Gelatine face paint step 2a.

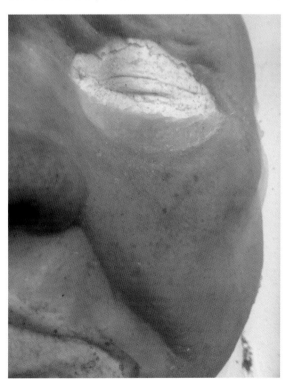

Gelatine face paint step 2b.

Gelatine face paint step 3a.

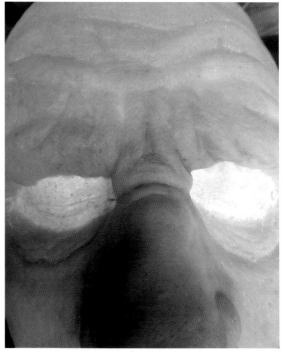

Gelatine face paint step 3c.

creating a soft airbrushed effect. This first step really helps the piece come alive and gives the impression of blood underneath the skin.

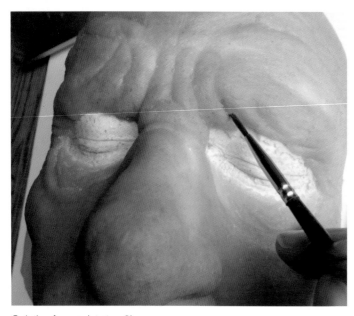

Gelatine face paint step 3b.

Step 3: Mix a solution of Blue Vein colour along with a medium brown and a little pink flesh to create the colour for the creases in the skin. Use a finer brush to let the paint flood into all these areas. You can start more heavily with the lines and move the paint with IPA. Keep this colour only in the creases, making it darker in some areas where you want the wrinkles to appear deeper.

Step 4: At this point spatter some more reds and freckle browns on the face to add more depth.

Step 5: The next stage is to add a few more shadows to the face using a pinky brown. Again keep the paint translucent, deposit it in the cheek areas and a little around the deep wrinkles in the eyes. Use the fluffy brush to diffuse any harsh edges.

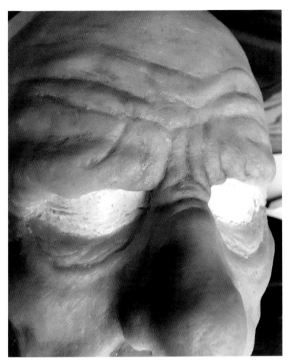

Gelatine face paint step 4.

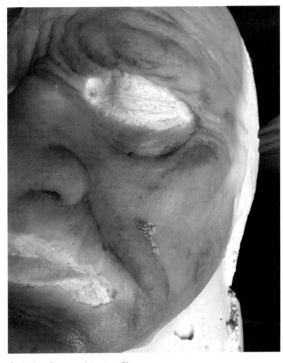

Gelatine face paint step 5b.

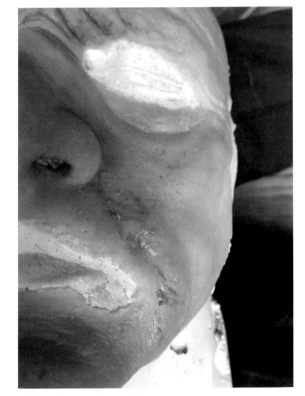

Gelatine face paint step 5a.

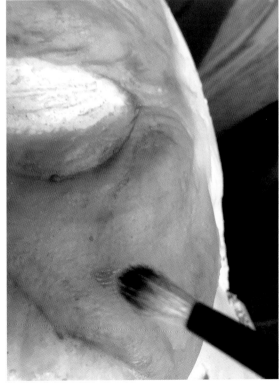

Gelatine face paint step 5c.

Step 6: Now you can have some fun with veins and broken capillaries. Using a fine brush and a very light touch, wiggle some veins very faintly in the temples of the forehead. Go lightly at first as you can always add more. Make sure the line is broken for more realism. Also using the fine brush, wiggle some broken capillaries around the nose and cheeks. A helpful tip is to use the end of a fine brush dipped in IPA to sharpen the edges of the veins by carefully running it along the end of the capillary. When creating fine veins and capillaries your work will look more realistic if you vary the opacity.

Gelatine face paint step 6b.

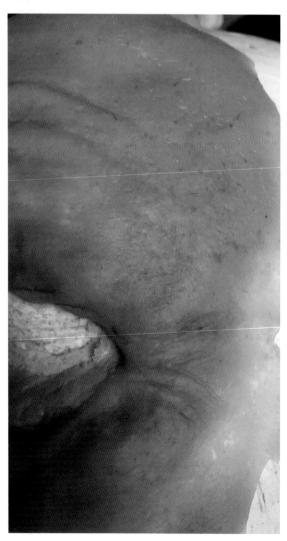

Gelatine face paint step 6a.

Gelatine face paint step 6c.

Step 7: Lastly, add a few age spots and moles for realism. You can then spray with a matt sealer such as Kryolan Fixing Spray or Ben Nye Final Seal.

Now the pre-paint is complete, let's move on to hair work.

HAIR PUNCHING CHARACTER EYEBROWS

In this section we will look at adding hair to our character. This will involve the addition of eyebrows and a beard. Here you will be introduced to two different techniques used by professional prosthetic artists.

First let's investigate how to punch hair, which is the art of taking an individual hair and embedding it into a prosthetic appliance using a forked needle. It sounds painful, so that is why we reserve this technique for fake heads and prosthetics that aren't attached to performers.

Materials and tools

- Fine beading needles – available at haberdashery or craft shops, size 10 works well
- Needle holder or pin vice holder – available at wig suppliers or online
- Small cutting snips – available at hardware stores
- Sharpening stone or slip stone – available at hardware or craft stores or online
- Chalk pen (optional). The example used here is a tailor's pen, which has a little wheel on the end and the inside is filled with chalk that makes a strong mark but can be wiped off. It is available at haberdashery stores or online. You could use a make-up pencil, but it's a little more difficult to remove without disturbing the underlying paint.
- Hair – real is best, either animal or human (you can use heat tools to style it, whereas most synthetic hair will melt)

- Sharp scissors
- Tweezers
- Eyebrow comb/clean mascara wand or toothbrush
- Gas torch and curling iron (optional)
- Hairspray (not pictured)

Hair punching equipment.

A chalk pen for hair punching.

Hair

Real hair is preferred over synthetic as you can heat style it. For eyebrows and beards you will find that yak, human and mohair work well. This can be found online and in some wig supply stores. This demo uses a mixture of yak and human hair. When you are working with hair you should know that it has a top and bottom, the root and the tip (the tip is the thinner end). It's important that you insert the hair root first so that it will lay correctly and will also be easier to style. You can buy wired cards (drawing cards/mats) to hold the hair and a tool called a hackle to mix different colours together. A hackle is like a mini bed of nails and must be used with care as it is extremely dangerous; it is also quite expensive. It isn't always necessary when beginning to learn the art of prosthetics to obtain each and every gadget. Spend your money wisely on materials and improvise rather than splashing out on some of the more extravagant tools, as you can always add to your tool collection as you go along. For this demo the hair will be mixed by hand. Simply keep separating it until all the colours are mixed. I've used a grey/white yak hair that contains some black hairs, and mixed in some auburn/light brown human hair.

Getting started

The first thing you need to do is decide on the shape you would like your brows to be. Look at some reference pictures. You will find that the eyebrow is a wondrous thing that comes in many shapes, sizes, colours, textures and lengths. Since this goblin is an older fellow, a fuller brow will give him more character.

It's important to study the direction in which the hair grows as this will help add realism to your character. Here the shape and direction of the hair has been drawn on. Draw on both sides before you add any hair, remembering that eyebrows don't need to be completely symmetrical: as the saying goes, 'eyebrows are siblings, not twins'.

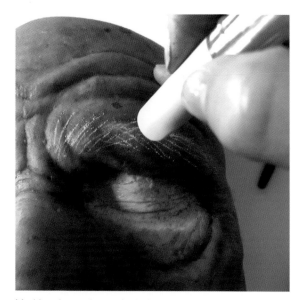

Marking the eyebrows for hair punching.

Next, and perhaps most importantly, you need to make a tool what will allow you to push the hair into the gelatine prosthetic. Most make-up FX artists make their own punching needle from a fine beading needle. Using snips, cut the beading needle at an angle as shown, and then use the sharpening stone to smooth off any burrs and make the needle as sharp as possible.

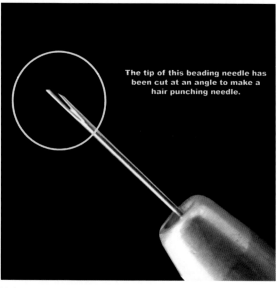

The tip of this beading needle has been cut at an angle to make a hair punching needle.

Hair punching needle.

Now you are armed with everything you need to start making eyebrows. This is a tricky process that requires a lot of practice and patience, but it will be worth the effort as, once you get the hang of it, it looks very realistic and gives the impression that the hair is actually growing out of the skin.

Take a few hairs in your hand and use the fork of the needle to separate one hair and push it into the skin. The fork will trap the hair, so that when the hair is pushed into the forehead the needle can be removed and the hair will stay behind as if by magic. No glue is required. The needle punctures the gelatine to allow the hair to enter, and as the needle is removed the hole returns to its original state as the gelatine relaxes, leaving the hair securely attached. Be sure to get only one hair in the hole as it will look more realistic. Use tweezers to remove any hairs that look out of place.

Note the angle of the hair in relation to the needle. The hair should always be held horizontal, while the needle is vertical. You will have to

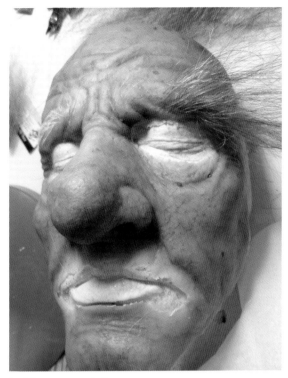

Building up more hairs.

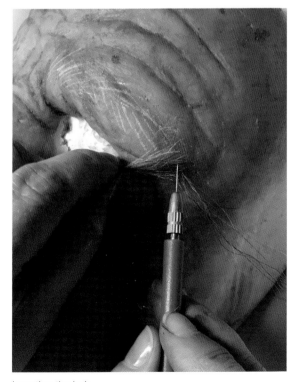

Inserting the hair.

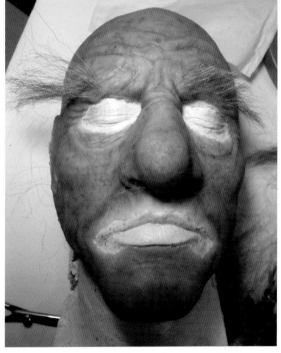

One eyebrow is now complete and the second is underway.

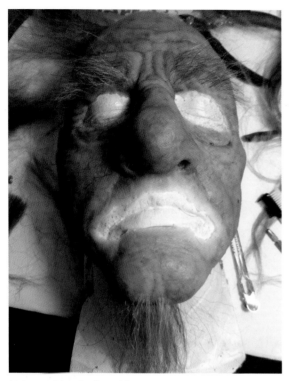

Hair punching the beard line.

alter your positioning as you work your way along the directional lines.

When you have completed one side you can start on the other. It may be helpful to turn the head upside down when it comes to inserting the second brow, as most people are right- or left-handed and usually find one side easier to work on.

When you have completed the brows you can also punch hair into the chin to create a beard. This character will have a full lower beard, so there is quite a lot of hair that needs to be attached. This is where the second technique comes into play. We will now look at hand-laying a beard.

HAND-LAYING A BEARD

To create the sides of the beard the hair will be laid and glued. This method is much quicker than punching each individual hair. It is also a better

technique to use on the sides of the face piece as the appliance is very thin here and there isn't a lot of material to punch the hair into. The tiny holes made by a needle can also weaken the thin piece. It is acceptable to do this and then punch the hair only along the inner edge when all the other hair has been glued down. This matches the aesthetic appeal of the other punched areas and looks like a real beard growing out of the cheeks.

Materials and tools

For this portion of the make-up you will need the following materials:

- Pros-Aide cream
- Sharp scissors
- Cotton tips or Q-tips
- Tweezers
- Eyebrow comb/clean mascara wand or tooth-brush
- Hair
- Isopropyl alcohol (IPA)

Getting started

Q-tips are used to apply the Pros-Aide. They are more efficient and clean up is easier as you won't have to get dried Pros-Aide off the brushes.

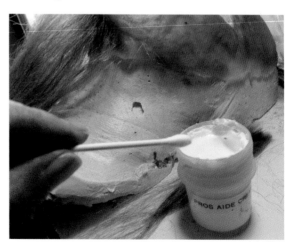

Beard laying using glue.

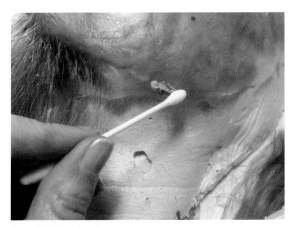

Beard laying glue line.

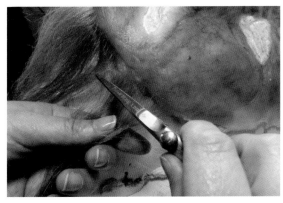

Press the hair into the glue using scissors.

The Pros-Aide is applied along the bottom edge of the face. You are going to glue a little section and stick some hair to that glue when it has dried clear and become invisible. Think about how bricks are laid in a pattern and adopt a similar strategy. Glue and hair can get messy very quickly, but by working in sections you can ensure a neat working area.

The hair should be cut blunt at the root end, leaving the tips long for now, as we will cut and style the hair later. Using the scissors, take the section of hair and press the root end into the glue.

Gently pull the hair back towards you. The excess will come away and the remainder will be secured to the face.

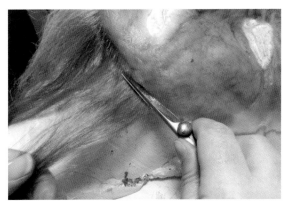

Pull away any excess hair.

Repeat this process until all the hair is glued down. Pay close attention to the direction you lay the hair, as you will want it to follow a natural growth pattern.

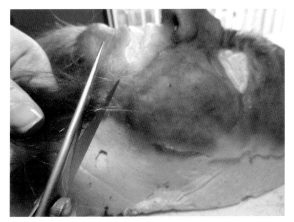

The hair for the beard should be cut level at the root end.

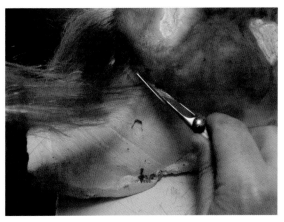

Continue laying the beard, still removing excess hair.

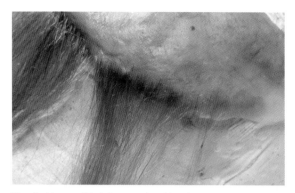

The first layer of hair is now glued in place.

Paint the next layer of glue slightly over the previous hairline. This will help secure it and blend in the new line.

Starting on the next layer.

Repeat the process on the other side, being careful to match the shapes on both sides. This doesn't need to match perfectly as asymmetry will look more natural.

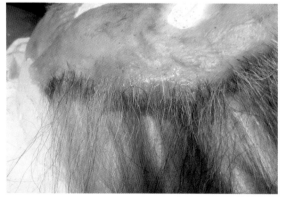

Repeat this process on the other side.

You can now soften the glued beard line by punching in the border hairs.

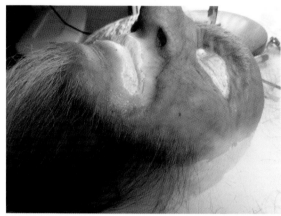

Punching in the border hairs.

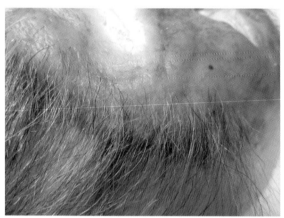

Use punched hair to break up the edge.

Styling the beard

When you are happy with the rough shape of the beard you can add a little finesse by cutting and curling it. Curling allows you to bend the hair and better position the direction it lies, helping you achieve a more natural look.

The type of beard tongs used for this purpose are an old-fashioned style used in Victorian and Edwardian times to curl real beards and hair. They are still available from wig and make-up stores, also sometimes at flea markets. They are still widely used today in the film industry.

Beard tongs are very thin. The most popular of the various types on the market are individual metal tongs that are heated in a purpose-built portable electric oven. The ovens are quite expensive, so here's a tip that offers the simplest, quickest and most cost-effective way of curling hair, even allowing you to use tongs on set or on location in the middle of nowhere without electricity. A blowtorch of the type used in the kitchen for making crème brûlée can be used to heat up the barrel of a thin beard tong. If you decide to use this technique you must exercise extreme caution, as you could get badly burned. This technique should only be carried out by responsible adults.

- There is a significant risk of burning either yourself or property.
- Never use this gas flame near flammable items.
- Keep the tong at arm's length when heating it, holding only onto the handle. Heat gloves can be used for added protection.

- Have a heatproof mat to rest the hot tong on. Be extremely careful where you set the hot tong.
- Never leave hot tongs unattended.

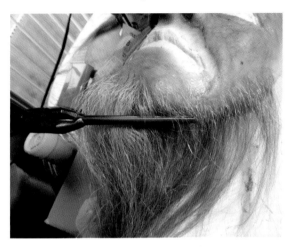

Hot tongs for styling beards.

Beard styling equipment.

The fully styled beard.

- You only need to heat it a little, as these types of tongs can easily burn hair, especially white or grey hair, which is more fragile. Test a little hair sample to see if the temperature is correct before you commit yourself to styling the prosthetic, potentially risking all your hard work.
- When curling the hair use a comb to protect the appliance, especially if it is made from gelatin, which will melt.

If all this sounds too risky, a comb and some hairspray will suffice.

As a finishing touch to the painting and hair work you could always add some nose hair.

HAND-LAYING HAIR ON OTHER MATERIALS

You can use these same hair-laying techniques on other materials as well. Indeed you can glue and lay hair directly onto someone's skin to create a beard. This is a technique strictly for professionals, however, as tonging a beard or moustache on someone's face is very risky and it's easy to burn them.

Practising on a gelatine face is a good idea as the gelatine will surely melt if touched by the hot tong. The gelatine also provides a realistic surface and will help you get into the habit of using the comb as a shield and stop you lingering in one area with the heat for too long.

It can be difficult to punch hair into foam latex, so for illustration purposes some pre-made RBFX foam latex ears were coloured to match this character and matching hair was laid on. This demonstrates that if you are careful and precise when laying hair you can make it look as good as punched hair on the face.

Curling the hair and twisting the ends with some styling wax gives the hair a good shape and really adds to the character. The addition of jewellery in the ears also adds more interest.

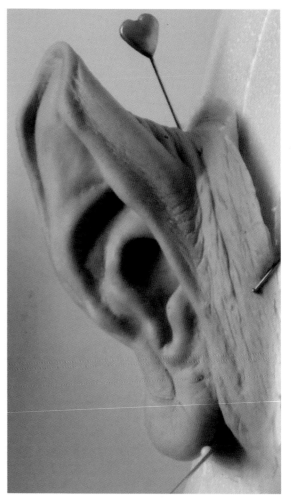

The original colour of the Goblin ear.

Adding paint and hair to the Goblin ears.

Laying hair on the Goblin ears.

Powdering down the Goblin ears.

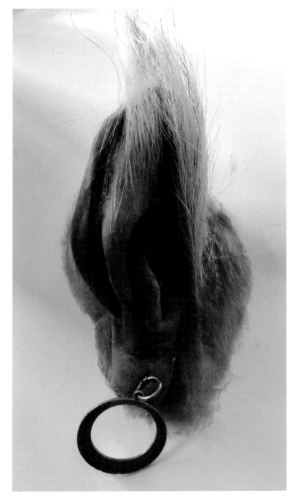

Applying some jewellery to the Goblin ears.

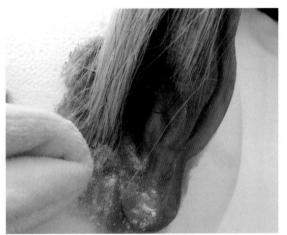

Using a powder puff to remove tack on the Goblin ears.

The completed Goblin ears.

8

APPLICATION AND REMOVAL OF PROSTHETIC APPLIANCES

After we have completed the pre-paint, hair work and ears for the character, we are ready to apply everything to our performer.

GOBLIN PROSTHETIC APPLICATION

Materials and tools

ABOVE: Appliances for applying prosthetics.

Materials used in applying prosthetics.

DISPOSABLES

- Tissues
- Wet wipes
- Cotton tips
- Cotton pads – large is best
- Hand sanitizer
- Drinking straws and bottled water for the performer
- Toothpicks
- Mints

HAIR PREPARATION

- Bald cap
- Water spritzer
- Kryolan Gafquat or Schwarzkopf Got2b Glued hair gel
- Acetone
- Comb
- Hairdryer

APPLICATION

- Prosthetic appliances
- Skin cleanser – you can use witch hazel or any other mild astringent to cleanse the skin
- Witch hazel – also used to blend edges of the gelatine appliance into the skin
- Telesis 5 adhesive and thinner – you could also use Pros-Aide
- Disposable cups, plastic shot glass or medicine cups for holding glue
- Glue brushes
- Mini flocked applicators – optional, but handy when you need to glue small areas
- Pros-Aide cream
- Cabo-patch/filler
- Spatula tool – small and flexible for filling edges
- Long-handled tweezers
- Small pointed scissors
- Hair scissors
- No-colour powder – RCMA or similar
- Powder brushes – large for face, smaller for eye area
- Powder puff
- Red rubber stipple sponge

- Fan – some people don't like the smell of glues and paints, so a fan might help. It's also useful for drying areas on a gelatine make-up

ART FINISHING (COLOURING)

- Alcohol-activated palettes
- Make-up brushes
- Cut-down chip brush
- IPA – Isopropyl alcohol (99%)
- Creme make-up (optional) – can be used around eyes
- Matt eye shadows in neutral colours – can be used around eyes
- Disposable or plastic artist's palette

ART FINISHING (HAIR)

- Tong for beard hair (optional) – a fine electric tong will also work
- Gas torch (optional)
- Comb
- Hairspray
- Hair accessories/jewellery

CLEAN UP

- Isopropyl myristate
- Small bowl for myristate
- Brushes – keep clean-up brushes separate
- Flannels
- Extra-large ziplock bags
- Microwave

Getting started

The very first thing you need to do is wash your hands. Make this a routine before doing any make-up, and do it when the performer is in the chair where they will see you. You are taking care of them and they will feel more trusting and comfortable if you show you are hygienic and considerate.

Next you need to apply a bald cap to the performer. This will protect the hair as well as give you something to stick the forehead section of the appliance to.

Applying a bald cap

Step 1: Prep your performer. Have them sit in a comfortable chair and make sure they are wearing an old shirt or you can put a protective cape over them. In this case the model is wearing a sleeveless T-shirt with a wide neck that can easily be pulled over the completed make-up or worn under the rest of the costume. It's important you consider this as you don't want to spend hours doing a make-up only to discover at the end they are wearing a personal shirt that cannot be pulled over their head without cutting it first.

Step 2: Next you will need to put a bald cap on the performer. Wet the performer's hair using a water spritzer, comb it back flat to their head and add Gafquat to flatten the hair. This has extreme hold on all types of hair, dries hard and is easily removed with shampoo and water. Use a hair-dryer to dry the Gafquat while pressing it down. If you can't get Gafquat, a good alternative is Got2b Glued water-resistant spiking gel (in the yellow tube). It is amazing stuff and readily available.

Step 3: Once the hair has been flattened to the head you can apply the bald cap. Here Telesis 5

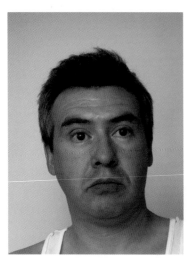
Prepping the performer.

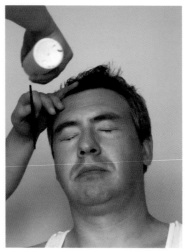
Wetting the performer's hair.

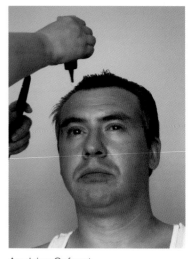
Applying Gafquat.

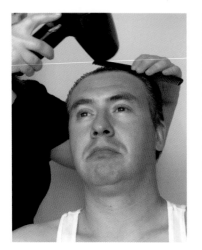
Blow dry the hair and flatten it.

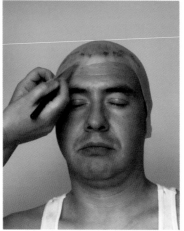
Applying the bald cap.

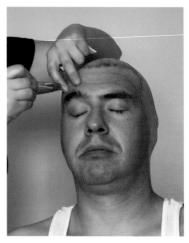
Apply glue to the eyebrows to flatten, powder when dry.

adhesive is being used. You could also use Pros-Aide, but if you do you should remember that Pros-Aide is a contact adhesive that needs to dry (clear) before you can successfully stick the prosthetic down. Once stuck it is more difficult to reposition if necessary. Telesis glues come with a solvent that can be used to lift and reposition a piece with ease. It is more expensive but can save a lot of time.

As this is a vinyl cap, the edges are blended away with acetone. Don't make extra work for yourself if the cap is to be covered by the prosthetic piece. Time is precious in the make-up chair and you don't want to keep the performer longer than necessary. For this particular make-up it isn't necessary to take the ears out of the bald cap, instead just cut some holes so the performer can hear.

Prepping and application

Step 4: Next you need to flatten the performer's eyebrows with the Telesis 5 glue. You will find that, particularly on men, their eyebrows can often come down underneath the appliance around the eye. This is not what you want as it will spoil the edge and look bad. It can also allow sweat to travel down into the eye. It's good practice to hold a cotton round over the eye area

when you do this to prevent glue dropping into the eye. Safety should always be first and foremost when applying prosthetics.

In order to reduce the possibility of glue dripping in any unwanted places, especially the eyes, make sure not to load your brush with too much glue. You should also squeeze the brush out by gently rubbing each side on a hard surface such as the sides of the glue cup or a disposable palette before putting it on the face. This is an especially important rule to follow when you are working around the brow bone as pressing an overloaded glue brush on this area can have a squeegee effect on the brush, causing excess glue to run out and potentially get into the eye, which is definitely not what you or the performer wants.

Another safety measure you can take is to put a little Vaseline on the eyelashes, which will prevent them sticking to any glued areas or to each other. The Vaseline should only be put on the eyelash hair and kept off the skin, as this can cause problems when you try gluing this area.

Step 5: This demo deals with a one-piece appliance, which is a little easier and faster to glue down than a seven-piece make-up. The technique used here is to glue all over the performer's face using Telesis 5 glue, leaving a little space

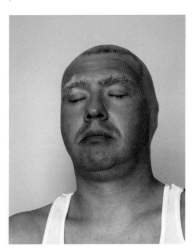

Powder the eyebrows.

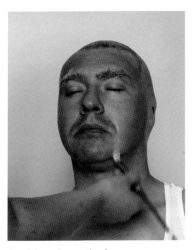

Applying glue to the face.

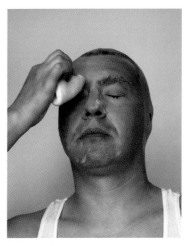

Powder all glued areas to remove tack.

around the eyes and mouth. Take care not to use too much glue where the prosthetic ends on these areas as the glued area can pick up dirt and lint. You should also leave a little so you can tweak these areas as necessary. Make sure the performer sits very still and keeps their face in a neutral expression for this process, as any movement can cause the face to stick to itself, especially around the creases of the eyes and mouth, so it's imperative to powder all the areas to which glue was applied with a powder puff and a substantial amount of powder. This will remove the tack. You should also do the same on the appliance, gluing it thoroughly and then powdering it. When you have pressed the powder in with a powder puff, use a fluffy brush to remove the excess powder. Never blow on the performer's face or your tools as it's unhygienic, unpleasant for the actor and unprofessional.

Step 6: Now that both the face and the appliance have been glued and powdered to remove the tackiness, you can offer the appliance up to the face. It's best if the performer tilts their head back slightly to allow easier placement of the piece. This piece has been custom made for the performer so it will lock on to their face with ease, using the nose and chin as the central

points to anchor it down. Make sure it's comfortable and that the mouth and eyes have suitable clearance. This particular piece is fairly heavy, so it's necessary to deal with the chin, nose and mouth first. The forehead has only been tacked for now and not fully pressed into place. This is to allow room to adjust the piece around the eyes. Even prosthetics that have been custom made can often sit heavily on the brow. You will want to allow some adjustment room here if you need to pull the forehead up a little (this will be further discussed later).

Prosthetics are often applied by two people and this is a lot easier than doing it by yourself. If necessary you can ask the performer to help you. If you start at the bottom and secure the chin, mouth area and nose, you can work your way up to the eyes and forehead. The pre-gluing that you have just done will, as if by magic, start to lock the piece down as it reactivates with the heat of the performer's skin. You can help it on its way by using a little IPA or Telesis 5 thinner on a brush. Go over the face carefully, adding pressure with your fingers, and you will find that it starts to stick by itself. If your character has facial hair like this one, a helpful tip is to clip any hair out of the way so you can see the edges of the appliance when gluing everything down.

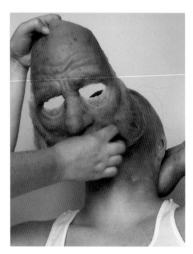

Once the piece has been pre-glued and powdered it can be offered up to the face.

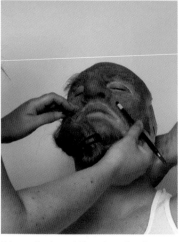

It is easier to put the piece in place if the performer's head is tilted back a little.

The edges are dissolved with witch hazel.

Step 7: Starting at the bottom of the piece, you can use the witch hazel to dissolve the fine edges of your piece. It melts gelatine very well. You will also need to seal these edges with Pros-Aide cream and a red rubber stippling sponge. These are invaluable tools that usually come as a circular synthetic sponge with a tight rubbery cellular structure. You can be frugal with these as you need only the tiniest piece. Dip it into the Pros-Aide cream and use a stippling motion along the edge of the prosthetic where it meets the skin. This will give a texture that is carried across both skin and prosthetic, tricking the eye into losing sight of the piece's edge. Your goal is to make it difficult for the audience to see where the prosthetic starts and finishes, and this tiny red sponge is the key to that. The sponges get spoiled after you use glue on them, so it's best to dispose of them, which is why you need only a tiny bit of sponge. A top tip is to use some long-handled tweezers to hold the sponge as you stipple. The Pros-Aide goes on as a thick white cream and dries clear. Remember that it is a glue and it will still remain sticky once dry, so it's important to powder it. The powdering also helps add texture to the area.

Step 8: Once you have stippled these areas, you can fill in any gaps using a thicker version of Pros-Aide cream commonly known as bondo or Cabo-patch, so named as it contains cabosil (fumed silica), which acts as a thickener. You can buy this ready made, but you can also make your own by mixing silica with Pros-Aide cream, making sure that you wear a mask as silica is dangerous when airborne.

Use a fine spatula to skim the material over any holes or crevices. You can also stipple over this to add texture if required. Another tip is to use a little water on a cotton tip to help blend the material and soften the edge.

As this is a thicker substance it takes a little longer to dry. If the prosthetic were made from silicone or foam latex we could utilize a hairdryer on a low heat to accelerate the cure time, but in this case you should remember that heat and gelatine don't mix well. Place a little on the chin and then move on to work on another area until the mouth area is dry. Just don't forget to come back and powder as Cabo-patch is still made from glue and will remain tacky – and as we've already stated, tacky areas pick up dirt quickly.

Step 9: Each prosthetic you work with may need a slightly different approach. This one is quite heavy as it is in one piece, which is why the nose, chin and mouth have been secured first. You will notice that the eyes are still a little loose,

Applying bondo to the edges.

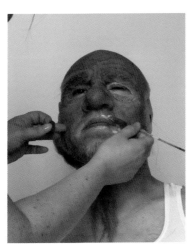

Smooth the bondo with a spatula.

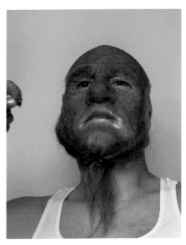

The bondo should be powdered to remove the tack.

but this is perfectly fine for now and we will get to them. As stated previously, the Telesis 5 thinner component can be used to reactivate areas that have been stuck down and manipulate them as necessary. Since the forehead has only been tacked down, we can now reactivate the glue a little, pulling up on the forehead piece to help get it into the correct position and making sure that it doesn't sit heavy on the eyelids and push the eyes closed. It's helpful to have a mirror in front of you when you are applying prosthetics to help you see the positioning of the piece. Don't pull too much on the piece as you don't want to distort it, but just keep it from pressing on the eyes.

Step 10: As stated earlier, leave enough space around the eye area to add the glue when you are ready. This helps you position the eyes correctly. If this area is already glued down when you pull up on the forehead it will stretch the eyelid upwards, giving the eye a strange look. Use very little glue on your brush at this point, as you don't want it to squeeze out and risk running into the eye.

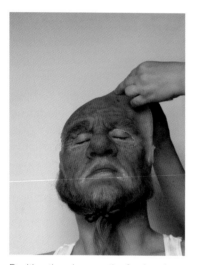

Position the piece on the forehead.

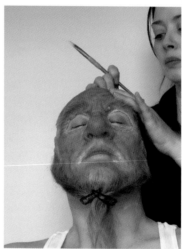

Glue the forehead into place.

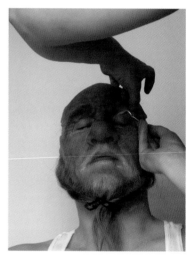

Adding glue around the eyes.

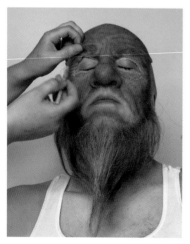

Lifting the eye area.

Secure the edges with Pros-Aide.

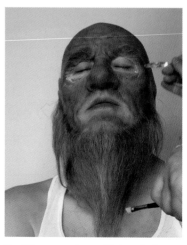

Seal the eye edges with bondo if required.

Using a disposable Q-tip saves clean up time.

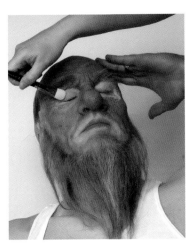
Powder the eyelids.

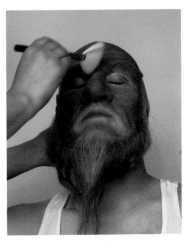
Remove excess powder.

Use the thicker part of the prosthetic to help you lift the edge up. Simply pressing or pinching this area will allow the edge to rise up and enable you to run the glue brush underneath.

Ask the performer to keep their eyes closed until you tell them it's safe to open, otherwise you risk sticking their eyes open. You may find that you won't need to put too much glue on the top lid as this can often look fine framing the eye, and it allows the eye to move freely, largely depending on the sculpt and the piece.

When you are happy with the eye area you can fill and seal the area as before with the Cabopatch and/or Pros-Aide cream. A cotton tip is often the best tool for this as it can be disposed of afterwards. It will also save time and effort getting Pros-Aide out of your make-up brushes. As before, remember to powder all of the areas you put the filler and Pros-Aide cream.

Step 11: In order to make the character more interesting we are adding a hat found in a costume store. It has been broken down a little by rubbing the edges with a rasp and adding some grime make-up to give it a lived-in look. It suits the character very well and allows you to create more interest by cutting some holes in the side and pulling the ears through. Again utilize a mirror to make sure the ears are level. You will notice there are still some areas on the face that need to be coloured. These have been left until the glue filler has dried. While this is happening, use the time to get on with other things, like fitting the hat and ears.

Applying prosthetics make-up is a lengthy process. Be considerate and have gum or mints available for both you and the performer, remembering that you are going to be pretty close to

Trying on accessories while allowing glue to dry on edges.

Marking the position of the ears.

Use a mirror to make sure the ears are level.

each other for a few hours. If they have been sitting for a while, let them have breaks to allow them to stretch and offer them water, but make sure there is a straw so you don't ruin the mouth edges.

Step 12: The great thing about being able to pre-paint pieces is that it cuts down the painting time immensely, which is beneficial to everyone involved. The final step that will pull your make-up together is to blend any areas that need it into the performer's skin. In this case you will need to concentrate on the areas of the mouth and eyes. Choose or mix a similar shade to the appliance and apply a very light wash. Next take the cut-down chip brush and splatter freckles over the skin, applying colours similar to those in the make-up. Try not to let this get too far onto the appliance as you are only marrying the two together. This simple technique will

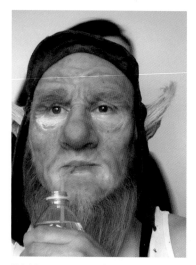

Drinking straws won't ruin your work when the performer needs a drink.

Using colour to blend the area around the mouth.

Adding colour around the eyes.

help blend the seams and further hide the edges of the appliance.

When you are working around the eyes, don't use alcohol-activated paints as they are too harsh and can irritate the eyes. Instead use matte eyeshadows and, if more colour is needed, use creme-based make-up. You can seal the cremes by using a no-colour powder or matte eyeshadow. Get the model to look up away from you when working around their eyes. To help steady your hand you can rest your finger lightly on top of a clean powder puff on their cheek; the puff will also help protect the paint.

Step 13: Dress the hair on the beard and ears, by using a little spray on your fingers and working it into the hair. This will help it hold its shape. The addition of ear and beard jewellery also adds character to the finished piece. It is attention to details like these that make a more aesthetically pleasing and interesting design.

You have now seen the entire process of making and applying a basic one-piece prosthetic appliance. Now it's your turn to have some fun with the techniques you have learned and see what you can come up with.

The drastic changes that simple three-dimensional make-up can make to a performer's natural appearance are strikingly apparent when you compare photographs from before and after. The reward for creating a make-up such as this becomes apparent when you see it come to life through the actor's performance.

When you are working around the eyes the performer should look up.

Dressing the hair on the ears.

Ear jewellery.

Dressing the beard jewellery.

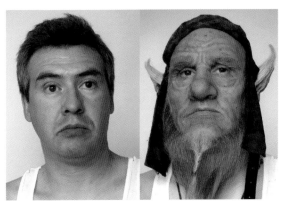

Before and after.

The completed Goblin character face.

PROSTHETIC MAKE-UP REMOVAL

It's important that you remove a prosthetic make-up with as much care as you applied it.

There are many types of remover on the market and the selection often depends on the type of adhesive you used. Two popular choices for removal are isopropyl myristate and Pro-clean. PPI, who makes the Telesis adhesives, also offers a remover for sensitive skin.

Most of the removers are oil based, which helps break down the glue. The trick to success-fully removing a prosthetic is to go slowly.

Materials and tools

- Prosthetic remover
- Cotton pads
- Wide medium-sized synthetic brush
- Bowl
- Tissues
- Wet wipes
- Flannels and small hand towel
- Microwave
- Ziplock bags
- Moisturizer
- Water spritzer
- Dry towel
- Powder puffs
- Individual eyedrops/individual saline drops

Step 1: Take the flannels and wet them. Wring out the excess water (leaving a little moisture), roll them up neatly and pop them in the micro-wave. You will need at least four per performer. Heat them up for about three minutes, but don't leave them unattended. Be extremely careful when taking them out of the microwave, using tongs as they will be very hot and can cause burns. You can pre-prep them by placing them in ziplock bags, but don't seal them fully when heating them up since you must leave a gap to let the air escape. They can be sealed after heating and will stay warm for some time.

Towels and prosthetic remover.

Step 2: You should set aside some brushes to be used exclusively for removal, because the oil in the remover can be difficult to remove from brushes. Even if they have been cleaned thoroughly you don't want the oil brushes to get mixed up with your glue brushes, just in case.

Keep a bowl exclusively for this purpose as well. Don't pour too much of the remover into the bowl. You don't need too much at a time and you will find you have to change it out a couple of times, so don't waste it.

Step 3: Start at the top of the prosthetic and work at an edge with the brush and some remover until it weakens and allows the brush to go underneath. It's better to make a smaller number of purposeful, yet gentle, swipes with the brush, since continually rubbing the same area over and over will cause irritation.

Get the performer to hold a few cotton pads or tissues over their eyes to help catch any stray drips. Be extremely careful when work-ing around the eyes not to load your brush with excessive remover in case it drips out and runs into the eye.

Find an edge that will weaken until the brush can enter.

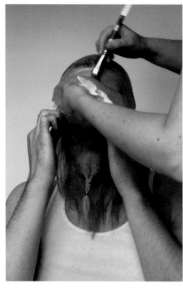

Work your way down the face.

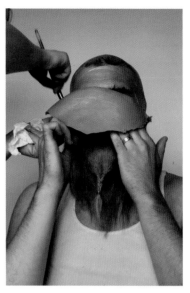

Get the performer to take the weight of the piece.

Step 4: Keep dipping the brush in the remover and working your way down the face, gently pulling the prosthetic out as you run the glue along the edge. This will help release it.

Get your performer to take the weight of the piece as it comes off their face.

Step 5: Once the prosthetic piece has been removed you can begin removing the glue from the skin, noting that there may still be a substantial amount left behind.

A powder puff works well as a removal tool. Get the performer involved in the removal

Almost there.

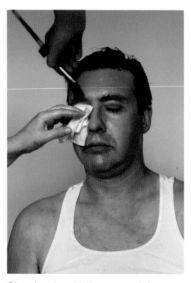

Cleaning the skin to remove leftover glue.

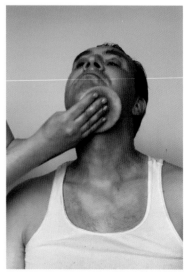

A powder puff can be used as a removal tool.

This is a job where the performer can join in.

Shake the hot towel.

Wrapping the face in a hot towel.

process, because they will rub their own face harder than you would dare.

Step 6: Everyone's favourite step is the hot towel – just don't make it the least favourite by burning your performer or yourself. Since it will still have a lot of moisture in it, there will be plenty of hot steam. Hold the towel by the very corners and shake it a few times. You can test the temperature on the inside of your arm before giving it to the performer. The towels cool off quickly, so don't shake them too much.

Step 7: Once the hot towel has done its work you can now apply some soothing moisturizing lotion or a barrier repair cream.

If only prosthetic transformations and removal were as easy as they make it look in the Mission Impossible movies! It's much more complicated and time consuming than that.

All clean!

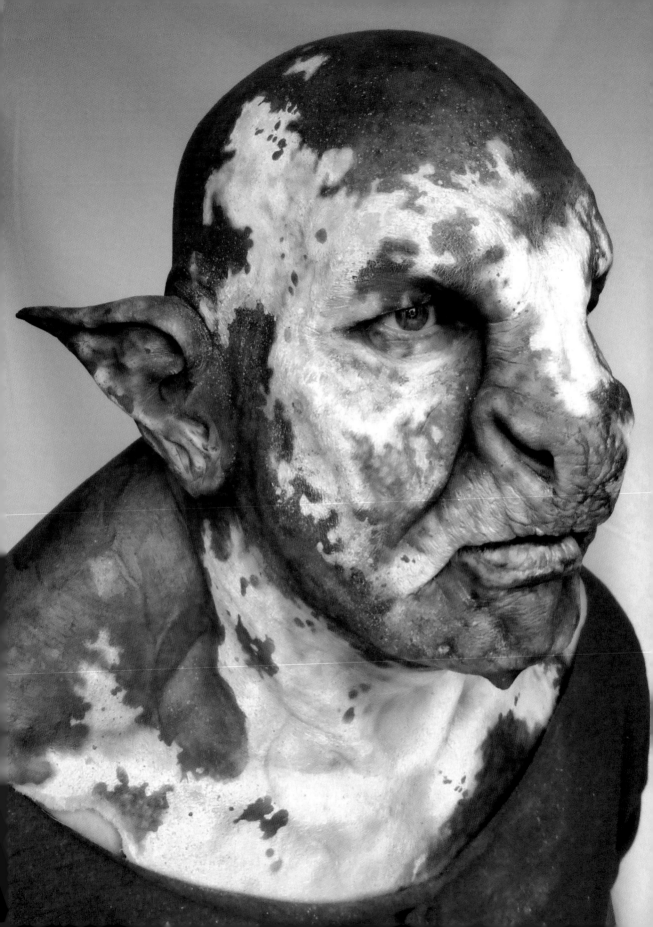

PART 3

CENTAUR CHARACTER: USING PRE-MADE PROSTHETICS

9

AIRBRUSHING AND DESIGN

This section of the book illustrates how a Centaur character is brought to life. Part 2 was all about making a prosthetic character from scratch. We will now deal with a pre-made generic appliance. These are made by other artists and are designed to fit a majority of people.

This time we are going to paint the character by airbrushing. Let's first look at everything that entails.

AIRBRUSHING

Airbrushing gives a smooth professional finish to your painting. You can cover large areas quickly. Shading from dark to light can be seamless and you can eliminate brush marks, resulting in an aesthetically pleasing paint job. With an airbrush you can use stencils and create effects such as beautifully detailed veins.

Airbrushing is also more hygienic as you don't have to keep washing make-up brushes between applications.

If you are thinking about adding an airbrush to your kit it can be quite overwhelming. It's an expensive purchase, but you will find that it opens up an endless range of possibilities and will be invaluable to your artistry.

Air compressor

You will need a compressor to power your airbrush. It basically works by sucking air from the atmosphere, compressing it and storing it in a chamber. This air is then released through an airbrush at a specified psi (pounds per square inch). When this pressurized air mixes with paint it has the effect of an atomizer, releasing a fine spray of tiny droplets of paint from the tip of the airbrush.

Compressors are available in all shapes and sizes, if you are considering purchasing one a good starter compressor is an Iwata

IS-850 Smart Jet, which is small, lightweight and powerful. Another workhorse is the IS-875 Smart Jet Pro.

Both of these air compressors come with an airbrush holder already attached. It is set up to use with an Iwata airbrush, but separate coupling adaptors are supplied to suit most airbrushes, including Aztek, Badger and Paasche models, so you can use your existing airbrush.

More importantly, these compressors also have built-in regulators and pressure gauges, which allow more control over the airflow. Obviously the more expensive the compressor the more features it will possess. Two features that will offer more control and a longer run time are the ability to set the air pressure higher and a larger air storage tank.

In order to decide on the best pressure setting for the compressor, get a piece of paper and play around with the pressure to see what happens. You will learn by practising. A good place to start is about 20psi, but you must take into account the drop in pressure when you activate the airbrush. Press and hold the air trigger on the airbrush when setting the regulator: as long as the paint is the correct consistency everything should work fine. Test the air on the back of your hand before you go near someone's face. You should lower the pressure when working on delicate areas of the face, especially around the eyes and mouth, as too much air could potentially blow them open.

A useful feature to have on a compressor is a moisture trap. Look for this when purchasing one. It helps remove moisture from the air hose and traps it in the glass vessel. This helps avoid surges of water coming through your airbrush that cause unwanted spatters as water mixes with the paint. Remember to press the release button on the moisture trap regularly to expel any water that builds up. You can also purchase mini moisture traps that fit directly on the air brush hose if your compressor doesn't have one.

Choosing an airbrush

The selection of airbrushes to choose from is mind boggling, so let's have a look at the jargon.

SINGLE ACTION

This type of airbrush employs a push on/off technique by which air is expelled via the button on top of the brush, much like a spray can.

These brushes are good for covering large areas and for spraying things such as cap plastic or thinned PAX paint.

They are also widely used for tanning as they give a steady spray. You have some control over the spray by selecting how close you are to the subject and by adjusting the air pressure. Some artists have developed a knack of doing this by bending the hose. It works – but perhaps might not be great for the longevity of the hose.

You can get this type of brush to spatter paint by adjusting the flow, but it takes some practice. The air supply in this type of brush is usually an external mix, so clean-up can be a little easier as the paint is mixed with the air outside the airbrush. They are usually fairly cheap. A recommended example is the Paasche H series single action, which comes with everything you need to get started. It's an excellent choice if you are going to want to spray cap plastic for encapsulated pieces or heavier viscosity paints, or if you need to achieve great spatter effects.

DOUBLE/DUAL ACTION

This type of airbrush has a dual-function button: pressing down gives you airflow, pulling back dispenses paint. You will have a lot more control with this type of gun as it has the advantage of enabling you to do very fine detail work as well as covering larger areas. This is further controlled by the distance to your subject.

Spatter effects can be achieved by either removing part of the nozzle or by altering the airflow. If you can only afford one airbrush go with a dual action. A competitively priced starter brush is the Evolution Silverline Two in One airbrush.

Another suggestion is the Iwata Hi-Line HP-CH airbrush, which is more expensive but a true workhorse, covering everything you could possibly need from an airbrush.

Feed systems

To add to the choices, you might be influenced by whether you require a gravity feed or siphon feed. The term feed describes how the paint travels through the airbrush and ultimately how the air and paint are mixed together. This can take place either outside of the airbrush (external feed) or on the inside (internal feed). The airbrush will have a vessel that holds the colour, from where it either flows downwards or is sucked up in the air chamber.

GRAVITY FEED

Also known as top feed, a gravity feed system is a popular choice for double-action airbrushes. It simply means that the cup which holds the paint is located on top of the airbrush; from here it is drawn down by gravity in an internal feed system to flow into the internal chamber of the airbrush, where it gets mixed with air.

Sometimes these cups are permanently attached to the airbrush, while others can be interchanged with cups of a different size. If you choose a model with a cup that is permanently attached, make sure it suits your purpose, because with this type of brush you will have to keep stopping to refill the cup.

Make sure the cup has a lid and always remember to use it: the last thing you want is to get carried away painting and accidentally spill paint on the performer's costume.

Gravity-fed airbrushes can usually handle heavier viscosity paints because, as the name suggests, gravity is used to transport the paint into the main chamber of the gun. This is another advantage of a top-fed airbrush since it requires less air pressure (again due to gravity).

SIPHON FEED

The main advantage of a siphon feed is the ability to interchange colour cups quickly. This will help save you time as you won't need to rinse the cup each time you need a new colour. They can also hold a lot of paint, which can be a huge advantage if you are going to be spraying large areas.

Siphon-fed brushes need more air pressure than gravity-fed models, as they have to work harder at pulling the paint up into the airbrush, this comes with a greater risk of creating unwanted over-spray.

SIDE FEED

This type of airbrush has a cup that fits on the side of the airbrush. This is useful as it allows more control of the angles you spray at. A variant of this has a swivel cup that rotates by itself depending on the angle you hold the brush. This is particularly useful if you need to spray at a vertical angle, eliminating the risk of paint spillage. A side-fed cup can also afford you unobstructed vision when you are painting (sometimes a gravity-fed cup can get in the way when you are doing fine close-up detail work).

Ultimately the choice of airbrush boils down to personal preference. Every type of airbrush will have its pros and cons, and your final choice will most likely depend on your budget and the application you intend to use it for.

Needles and nozzles

There are three main sizes of needle used in prosthetics airbrush application:

1 (fine). Used for fine detail work, paint going through this type of needle is thinner in consistency.
3 (medium). A good general-purpose needle that sits somewhere in the middle. It will handle most of your make-up needs.
5 (heavy). This needle is designed for more viscous paint, and materials like PAX and cap plastic.

It's important to note that each needle fits into a corresponding nozzle, so you need to make sure you have both. When you purchase an airbrush it generally comes with a no. 3 needle. You can usually identify the needle size by counting the rings machined around the top end of the needle.

Paint medium

When you are using an airbrush for make-up that will go on an actor's skin, you have a wide selection of pre-mixed colours and manufacturers to choose from. These will be water, silicone or alcohol based.

Remember to shake the colours really well as the pigment may settle to the bottom. A top tip is to put a small ball bearing inside to help agitate the mix. An even more important tip, however, is to make sure you secure the twist top when you are done. It's easy to forget and it can be disastrous when you pick up a bottle that was opened previously, shake it vigorously and its contents goes everywhere!

Your paint selection will depend on the application. Alcohol inks are a popular choice as the liquid colours correspond with the alcohol-activated palettes. This can be useful as the dried palettes are great to pop in your on-set make-up kit.

They are also considered skin safe (but you should always test a patch first). These are the inks used throughout the demos in this book.

If you are painting a mask or a creature, FW inks from Daler Rowney are a cheaper alternative. They have great pigment and are flexible and hard wearing, whereas silicone-based inks are great for blending prosthetics into female skin.

No matter what type of medium you decide to use you will quickly discover that you need to clean your airbrush thoroughly at the end of each session.

The next section will explain step by step how to take an airbrush apart. Your brush may be slightly different to the one shown, perhaps with more or fewer parts, but the basic principle will be the same.

Getting to know your airbrush

The model we will be dissecting, cleaning and putting back together is the Iwata Hi-Line HP-CH airbrush. You should literally get to know your airbrush inside out. It is a precision instrument and was probably quite an expensive purchase, so you need to learn how to take care of it if you are to have a long and happy life together.

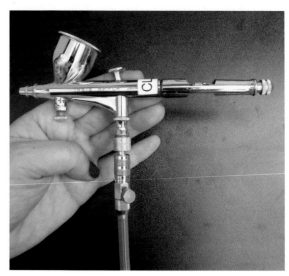

Iwata Hi-Line HP-CH airbrush.

The exploded view of the airbrush included here is fully labelled so you can identify all the parts. A good tip when you take your airbrush apart is to photograph every stage. Use a tray or contained space where all the components will be safe and not roll off the edge of the surface and onto the floor. You might need to dismantle it a couple of times before you get to know each component and how it fits together.

MATERIALS AND TOOLS FOR KEEPING YOUR AIRBRUSH CLEAN
- IPA Isopropyl alcohol
- Airbrush cleaning spoolie tools

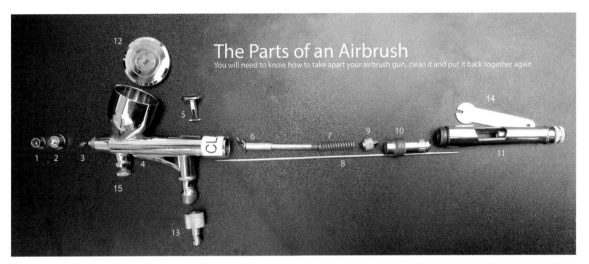

Exploded view of the Iwata Hi-Line HP-CH airbrush: (1) needle cap; (2) nozzle cap; (3) fluid nozzle (don't lose this as it's expensive and difficult to replace); (4) main body; (5) main lever; (6) needle chucking guide; (7) spring; (8) needle; (9) needle chucking nut; (10) spring guide; (11) pre-set cutaway handle; (12) cup lid; (13) quick-release valve (add-on item); (14) spanner/wrench; (15) micro air control valve.

- Airbrush lubricant
- 1 large pot (big enough to submerge the airbrush in it)
- 1 flat tray or dish to hold safely all the components that need soaking
- 1 small cup to keep small components you wish to keep dry
- Kitchen towel

TAKING THE AIRBRUSH APART

Let's start by looking at the sequence of pictures illustrating the parts. The smallest part of this airbrush is the fluid nozzle. Some artists don't always remove this when cleaning their brush, but you will obtain much better results by taking a little more time and effort and making sure it's clean. Leave it to soak somewhere safe, before holding it between your fingers and cleaning it thoroughly. The reason this is important is because this is the worst offender for blockages in this type of brush. Not every airbrush has something like this, but if your model does it

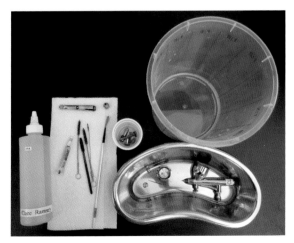

Equipment for cleaning an airbrush.

The smallest part is the fluid nozzle.

Special spanner to fit the fluid nozzle.

Cleaning inside the airbrush.

Fluid nozzle removed.

Getting inside the cup with a brush dipped in IPA.

should also come with a small spanner that fits it perfectly. It is essential that you keep both the nozzle and the spanner safe.

CLEANING INSIDE THE AIRBRUSH

Another important reason for removing this tiny nozzle is that it will now allow access into the chamber of the airbrush using a specially designed spoolie tool dipped in IPA.

If your airbrush has detachable cups these can be removed for soaking. If they are fixed, however, like this one, you can use a brush dipped in IPA to get down inside the cup to dislodge any residual paint.

BLOWING IPA THROUGH THE AIRBRUSH

Another great tip is to fill a deep pot with enough IPA that will allow you to submerge your airbrush in it. Ensure the tip and cup are fully covered and, while you have it attached to an air hose, press the trigger. This will cause bubbles and the effervescent effect will really help clean your airbrush.

Blowing IPA through the airbrush.

CHOOSING THE CORRECT CLEANING TOOLS

When cleaning an airbrush it is best to never use a cotton bud or pipe cleaner, even though these are sometimes sold as part of airbrush cleaning equipment, because the fibres can come off and block the airbrush. Metal spoolie brushes are much better for this, as is a long rigger artist's brush, as the fibres won't come off. Another useful (and fearsome-looking) tool is an airbrush reamer, which is a small metal tool designed to clear nozzles that have become blocked with dried paint.

Airbrush reamer.

REASSEMBLING THE AIRBRUSH

Once you have cleaned the airbrush you need to put it back to together. Start with the tiny fluid nozzle, which should be tightened with the spanner as far as the term 'lucky tight' suggests. Then assemble the other parts of the nozzle in order. It's a good idea to put the small parts back together as soon as possible so they don't get lost.

The dismantled nozzle.

Reassembling the nozzle.

The completed nozzle.

CORRECT LEVER INSTALMENT

If you dismantled the lever section, it's next on the list. Make sure you know the correct way to put it in the hole as it can be a bit fiddly and it's slightly different on every model. You can usually tell that it's in the correct position by looking at the texture on the part where you place your finger. It should be raised slightly towards the back to give it a more ergonomic design. Make sure that it pushes down easily to activate the air.

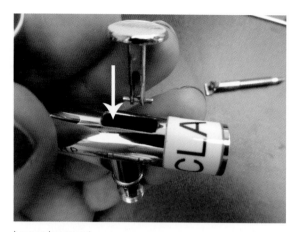

Lever placement.

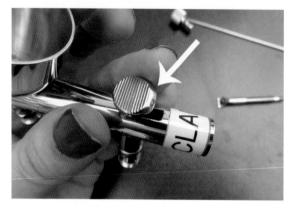

Note the direction of the moulded texture.

REPLACING THE SPRING

Next position the spring onto the needle chucking guide. Insert this into the main body of the airbrush, making sure the rest is tight up against the trigger.

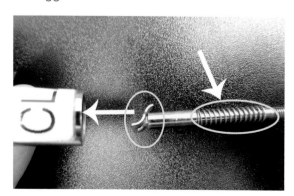

Trigger spring.

Push up the spring lever.

Now insert the spring guide and screw it into place.

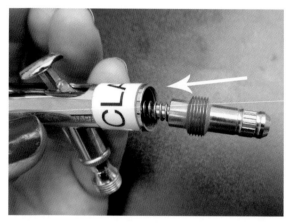

Screw the spring guide into place.

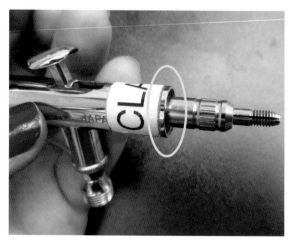

Tighten the spring guide.

INSERTING THE SPRING

You should now very carefully insert the needle. You must take the utmost care of your needle as it is arguably the most important part of your airbrush. If it gets bent your airbrush won't work to its optimum capability. Needles are relatively cheap to replace, but they can get damaged by dropping the airbrush or by inserting it incorrectly when reattaching the parts. Some artists don't like anyone else to touch their airbrushes as they are expensive precision instruments. It can be a pain if they stop performing as they should for no apparent reason. You can easily damage someone else's brush if you offer to clean it but are not experienced or as careful as its owner. Always be respectful and ask permission first. This goes for any equipment belonging to others.

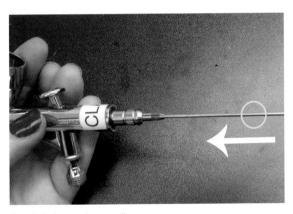

Carefully insert the needle.

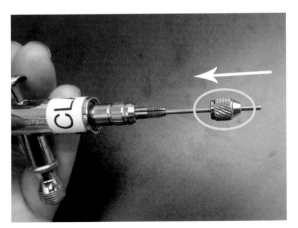

Screw on the needle nut.

ADDING THE HANDLE

Be extremely careful with this next step too, as you can easily bend the tail of the needle. If your airbrush has a pre-set cutaway handle, like this one, make sure the part that holds the needle is lined up properly before you try to screw it together.

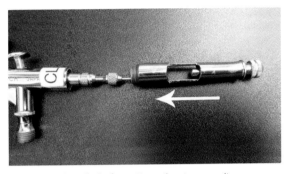

Line up the handle before attempting to screw it on.

Screw the handle into position.

QUICK RELEASE ATTACHMENTS

This airbrush has an additional piece added to the screw threads to which the hose is normally attached. This is a quick release valve and it has a corresponding part that fits onto the hose itself. This allows you to quickly change over to another airbrush fitted with the same attachment. This is a useful feature that can save a little time.

The little dial that can be seen on the photograph of a hose pipe is an air regulator, a feature that is not found on the more basic hoses. This particular airbrush also has a tiny air regulator positioned under the cup.

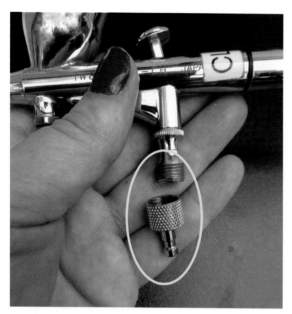

Attaching the optional quick release.

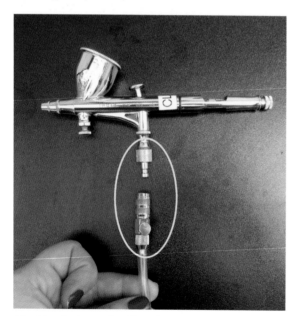

Attaching the hose pipe. Note the dial of the air regulator.

Essential extras

Before we leave the topic of airbrush equipment, let's look at two more items that are useful to have in your kit. The first one is a cleaning pot, which is particularly useful as it allows you to blow excess

paint or IPA into the chamber, preventing it from entering the atmosphere and getting breathed in. Airbrushing causes a mist that lingers in the air, especially when you are cleaning it out with cleaner or IPA, so when you are about to clean the chamber of the airbrush you need to get rid of the excess spray. This is where this convenient and portable glass pot comes into play. It has a small replaceable sponge filter on the side and it eliminates overspray when cleaning the airbrush, which is something anyone you are

Cleaning pot.

Cleaning pot holder.

Roll of PTFE tape.

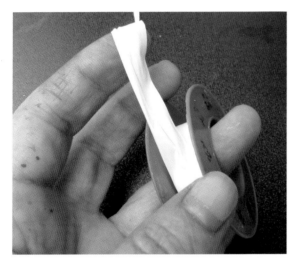

PTFE tape.

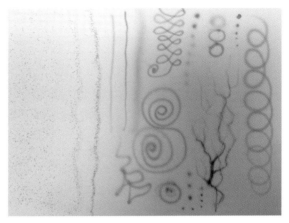

Airbrush techniques.

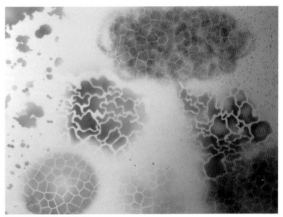

Airbrush stencil results.

sharing a small make-up truck with will thank you for. This cleaning pot also has the added advantage of a built-in airbrush holder.

One last thing you should have in your kit is some PTFE thread seal tape of the type used in plumbing. This is a flexible thin plastic tape that can be wound around the coupling of the compressor and will fix the problem if you hear any air leaks.

Practise with your airbrush to see what type of effects you can get by altering the air pressure or removing the tip, a feature only available on some brushes. If you remove the tip, be careful as the paint can leak out. You can get an effective spatter pattern with the tip removed on some of

the Iwata brushes. You can also experiment with stencils. A finely crafted piece of equipment such as the airbrush will surely inspire your creativity.

USING COMPUTERS AS A DESIGN TOOL

In this section we are going to take a brief look at using a computer as a tool when it comes to designing paint schemes for prosthetic make-up. This isn't a lesson on Photoshop, but simply illustrates some possibilities.

Photo editing software, such as Photoshop, can be incredibly helpful in showing you what

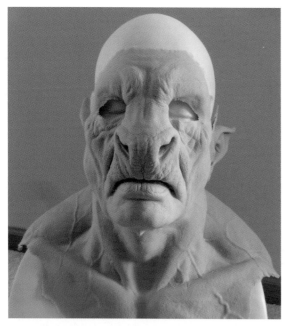

Centaur design mounted onto a bust.

a paint scheme might look like before you actually commit to putting paint onto a prosthetic appliance. It also means you can change things around without having to use up a lot of appliances. These can be costly to make and you will now be aware how much time and effort is involved in manufacturing them.

Computers, in general, and the Internet affords you access to a wealth of knowledge and reference material. You can use elements of nature, animals, flora and textures as inspiration for your designs. Everything is right there at your fingertips.

A prosthetic effects artist will often be given a design to copy that has already gone through a design process. You will be confined to the constraints of this design, whereas if you are designing your own character you will have a lot more free rein. Prospective employers will want to see your personal work to judge the range of your imagination.

It's also worth knowing that you don't always have to make your own prosthetics as there are companies that supply pieces you can incorporate into your own designs. These are known as 'generic' appliances and are designed to fit the majority of people.

The sources range from hobbyists selling their small prosthetics online to professional prosthetic workshops producing high-end film quality appliances. The centaur character included here is made up of three different

Browsing the RBFX online catalogue.

Photoshop is used to copy and paste the nose of a real horse onto the face piece.

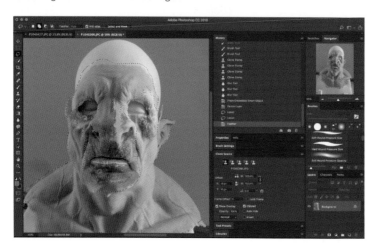

RBFX appliances chosen from the company's online catalogue: a face piece, a neck and a set of ears. They come from a huge selection of designs that you can easily mix and match to create interesting characters. For more details on where you can find these items, see the list of suppliers towards the end of the book.

It's also worth checking out the galleries of other artists' work, but it's important to remember to look at their work for inspiration, and never to copy or steal their ideas. Don't take the credit if it's not all your own effort, and share credits if you were assisted.

The unpainted face piece is first mounted on a bust to enable a detailed photograph to be taken in good lighting conditions. The photo is then transferred to the computer.

The design concept was to turn this piece into a centaur (half man, half horse) based on a brown and white American Paint Horse. These are stunning animals and provided the inspiration for this paint scheme.

The first thing you need to do is gather a few images that have the flavour of your proposed design. You can then start digitally copying elements from images of real horses and pasting them on the prosthetic photo, starting with the nose.

Working in Photoshop you can twist and flip the images to fit the desired shape. You don't need to be particularly skilled, either, and fast, effective results can be achieved with a few basic tools.

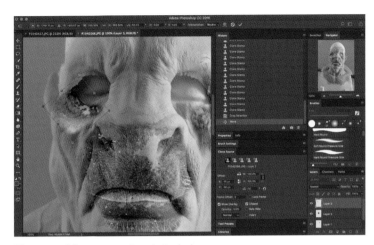
Close-up of the copy and paste technique.

Colour balance.

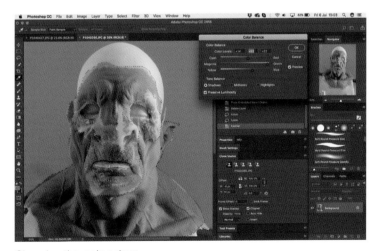
Changing the main colour.

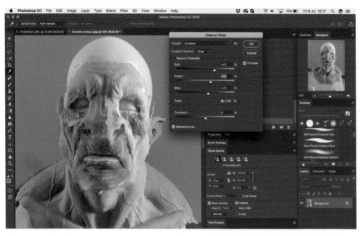

Colour variations.

Research will help show the texture of a horse's coat.

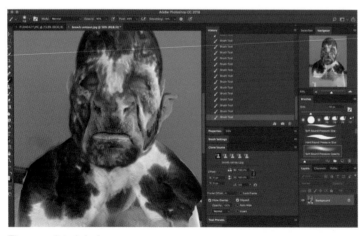

The completed design.

Next the main shape of the head is selected using the lasso tool. The colour balance tool is then used to alter the overall colour, taking it from a pinky tone to chestnut.

The colour selected can then be tweaked to see how another colour might look. In this case a grey tone was used instead of the brown, as it made a better underpaint colour. This can then be enhanced and darkened with shades of brown.

More photo reference material, such as details of the breed's coat, can be pulled from the Internet and manipulated to fit with the design.

The competed design shows how other shades of brown can be used to tie everything together. A professional Photoshop artist could turn this into a stunning picture, but this exercise was intended to see if the idea for the paint scheme will work on the prosthetic, and it has served that purpose well. It is now time to move on to painting the real thing.

In this chapter we have learned about airbrushes and computer design. Next we are going to take our airbrush knowledge and apply it, translating the digital design into a paint scheme and bringing it to life on the foam latex appliances.

10
PAINTING AND APPLYING FOAM LATEX

In this chapter we are going to paint a different type of prosthetic material, foam latex, which is unlike gelatine or silicone in that it is opaque. It doesn't have the same translucent quality of the other two materials and this makes it slightly more challenging to paint.

Materials and tools

- Foam latex appliances
- Long ball-headed pins
- PAX – acrylic colours mixed with Pros-Aide adhesive
- Bath sponge or sponge wedges
- Brushes
- Mixing sticks
- Cotton tips/q-tips
- Stencils
- Cut-down chip brush
- No-colour powder
- IPA – Isopropyl alcohol (99%)
- Alcohol-activated ink palettes and liquid ink

Painting foam latex materials.

- Airbrush gun
- Air compressor
- A form to pin the appliances to, such as a polystyrene head

FOAM LATEX AND PAX PAINT

The special type of paint we are going to make for use with the foam latex is called PAX and has long been used in the make-up effects industry. You can buy it ready made, but it's really very simple to make your own and this will give you more control over the colour and amount you need. It's non-toxic and is therefore safe to use directly on skin, which is helpful when you are blending prosthetic edges. PAX is also great for covering tattoos.

PAX can be tricky to remove, however, so think carefully where you are planning to use it. Don't put it close to the eyes and be aware of the problems with putting it on areas with a lot of body hair, including arms and chests. It would be advisable to shave these areas first, as the hair will otherwise give it an odd appearance and removal could be painful.

Making your own PAX paint

PAX is made by mixing a 1:1 ratio of Pros-Aide adhesive to acrylic paint. Liquitex is a popular brand of paint for this, though other brands can also be used. The addition of the glue gives the paint a flexible quality that allows it to stick to the soft, flexible, foam latex appliance. As it is made from an adhesive you will need to powder it thoroughly since it will dry with a sticky, shiny coating. The powder will help to remove the tack and eliminate the shine.

Another technique is to leave the shine and tack on the PAX paint and then go in with alcohol ink air brush colours, which will stick nicely to the PAX layer. This will be the technique used here to paint the centaur make-up. You can also airbrush PAX paint, but you will need to thin it as it can clog your airbrush quickly. Remember that when using your airbrush, whatever the medium, you should always do it in a well-ventilated area and wear a mask.

Applying PAX paint

The best application tool for PAX paint is a soft sponge, such as a fine-pored bath sponge. You could also tear a foam make-up wedge apart to expose the sponge's texture. You will want to keep the edges of the sponge rounded to eliminate square prints when dabbing paint on the appliance.

This is a sticky process and you will work more efficiently if you wear protective gloves. A good tip is to wear gloves that are a size smaller, as this will give you a better fit and the fingertips won't start to loosen and stick to themselves.

PAX will stick to your regular brushes, so use disposable sponges, Q-tips or cheap art brushes. You can aid the clean up by rinsing them in water as you go along. They can also be cleaned with IPA, but it will be difficult and time-consuming to remove all the PAX from a brush.

PAX is opaque, which means it's a solid colour. You can help make it a little more translucent by creating a PAX medium, which is a mixture of Pros-Aide and liquid matt acrylic medium. This will essentially act as a thinner that you can add in varying amounts to the PAX colours, essentially thinning them in much the same way you would use water to thin regular acrylic paint and achieve varying degrees of translucency. This is useful when it comes to painting skin tones with PAX as it will even allow you to spatter with a chip brush.

Since this creature has the patterns of a horse's coat, we are going to approach the painting with straight PAX (no medium has been used to thin the paint). Instead the depth will be built up by airbrushing tonal variations.

Step 1: Find something you can securely pin your prosthetics onto. Mix up the PAX colours

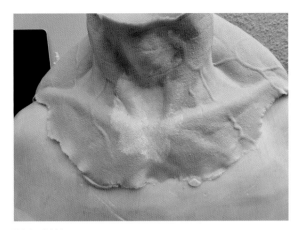

White PAX.

Applying white PAX on the face.

Applying white PAX on the neck and chest.

IPA. Always test spray on some tissue or paper to check the flow before you move on to the prosthetic. You will be using the airbrush along with stencils. This will take some concentration and you may have to work in reverse to get the pattern you are trying to achieve. In the photo here, for example, the pattern will work better if the stencil

you are going to need in small disposable cups. If you do this in a small jar with a lid, you will be able to keep some that will match perfectly when you come to applying the make-up.

Start by stippling the mixture of white PAX paint on to the neck area. Keep it thin and build it up gradually, leaving the very edges of each appliance bare. This will help you glue them down later, as they will be soft and pliable.

Step 2: Do the same on the face area. Note how the eye area has been left bare.

Step 3: Once you have laid down a layer of PAX you can begin airbrushing with alcohol inks, which can be thinned as necessary with more

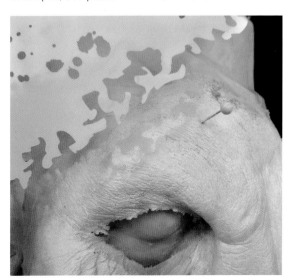

Using stencils.

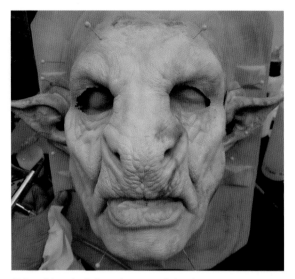

Airbrushing the lightest brown, a light chestnut.

is flipped around. The final look you will be after uses a combination of freehand airbrushing and stencils. Start with lighter tones and work your way up to darker colours.

Step 4: After you have worked out a rough shape with the light chestnut colour you can confidently move on to a darker colour. If you remember from the description of the digital designs, the under-colour was grey, so we are going to mimic this in the paint job. When you lay down this grey underpaint you can then go back in with a trans-lucent chestnut colour, which will allow some of the shadows of the underpaint to show through.

Applying grey underpaint.

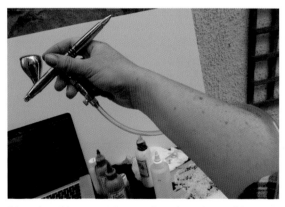

Wrap the tubing around your wrist to keep it out of the way.

Airbrush on browns and dark greys.

Step 5: You can now introduce darker brown tones by adding darker grey. Simply copy the digital paint scheme that had already been laid out until you are happy. Bear in mind that you mustn't fully finish the paintwork on the face at this point as you need to leave some room to add more paint to blend in your edges later when you come to apply the make-up.

Step 6: You will need to bring similar detailing to the neck area of your appliance, using your airbrush and stencil to create interesting effects.

The pre-paint is almost complete. You will need to do the ears as well and thoroughly powder everything to eliminate the sticky surface. Now all you need is a model.

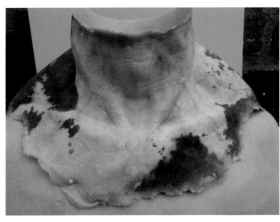
Add details to the neck.

FOAM LATEX APPLIANCE APPLICATION

Materials and tools

DISPOSABLES
- Tissues
- Wet wipes
- Cotton tips
- Cotton pads – large is best
- Hand sanitizer
- Drinking straws and bottle water for the performer
- Toothpicks
- Mints

HAIR PREP
- Mirror
- Beard trimmer
- IPA or other antiseptic spray
- Bald cap
- Water spritzer
- Gafquat or Got2b Glued spiked hair gel
- Acetone
- Comb
- Hairdryer

APPLICATION
- Foam latex prosthetic appliances

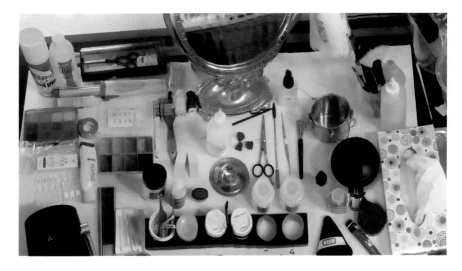
Foam latex appliance materials.

- Skin cleanser – witch hazel or any other astringent
- Telesis 5 adhesive and thinner or Pros-Aide
- Disposable cups, plastic shot glass or medicine cups for holding glue
- Glue brushes
- Mini flocked applicators (optional) – handy for when your need to glue small areas
- Pros-Aide cream
- Cabo-patch/filler
- Spatula tool – small, for filling edges
- Long-handled tweezers
- Small pointed scissors
- Hair scissors
- No-colour powder – RCMA or similar
- Powder brushes – large for face, smaller for eye area
- Powder puff
- Red rubber stipple sponge
- Fan – especially for use with those who don't like the smell of glues and paints

ART FINISHING (COLOURING)
- PAX paint – Pros-Aide plus the acrylic colours you need to mix into it
- Sponge wedges
- Alcohol-activated palettes
- Make-up brushes
- Cut-down chip brush
- IPA – Isopropyl alcohol (99%)
- Creme make-up (optional)
- Matt eyeshadows in neutral colours
- Disposable or plastic artist's palette

ART FINISHING (HAIR)
- Comb
- Toupé tape (optional)
- Hairspray
- Hairpiece (optional)
- Hair accessories, clips and feathers

CLEAN UP
- Isopropyl myristate
- Small bowl for myristate
- Brushes – keep clean-up brushes separate

- Flannels
- Extra-large ziplock bags
- Microwave

Getting started

This application will be conducted in much the same way as the gelatine piece, although there are a few elements that may differ slightly. You may want to refer back to some of the earlier chapters for more details on certain elements.

This time we have the addition of a neck piece that is rather large and must be placed over the performer's head. If you were doing this make-up for a film production the actor would most likely arrive wearing the under-section of their costume, as once this neck piece is in place it will be extremely difficult to get a T-shirt over it without putting the make-up at risk. If they don't have anything suitable you may have to provide them with a shirt that can be cut at the neck. It's important to be aware of the actor's comfort: not everyone wants to sit shirtless for hours, so be prepared and inform the costume department of your needs, if necessary.

Here a large T-shirt has been provided that can be cut at the neck to suit the purpose.

The make-ups in this book have been completed in various locations. This one was done in a kitchen, but with the added luxury of a tall make-up chair, which definitely helps save your back. After a time performing make-ups you will become aware of the jaunty angles you may find yourself adopting while doing applications. You have to be aware of the long-term effects of this, as it can play havoc with your back. These tall chairs are life savers. When you are applying bald caps or doing other hair work you will want to have the performer sit in a lower chair as this makes it easier to work on the top of their head.

Normally a professional make-up truck is fitted with chairs that can be adjusted to the height of the performer, which can be helpful considering the long application times.

Step 1: Prep the performer and have them change into a suitable shirt. The cape will be used to cover his legs to save his clothing from any potential glue drips. You will now have to apply a bald cap, which will be seen on this occasion. The edges, however, will still be covered, so there is no need to worry about blending them too much (please refer back to Chapter 4 for detailed information). The neck piece has been pulled on over the performer's head. Since it is foam latex it will be stretchy. The bald cap was then applied. If you wish you could do the bald cap first, but the one being used on this occasion was quite thin, and the fear was that it might tear when the neck piece was pulled on.

Using a bald cap has the advantage of giving you extra surface area to which you can stick the forehead piece. The prosthetic face piece can then be offered up to the performer's face to check the fit. The edge is then marked out with a powder puff that has been dipped in powder.

You need to press the powder just over the edge of the appliance so that when you lift off the appliance you will be left with a powder line. This is a good trick to discover how far you can put the glue or paint. You never want to glue past where the appliance sits as this can cause

Cut the shirt as necessary and pull on the neck piece.

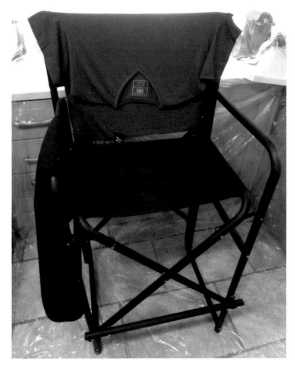

The choice of chair, shirt and cape make the job more comfortable and protect the performer's costume.

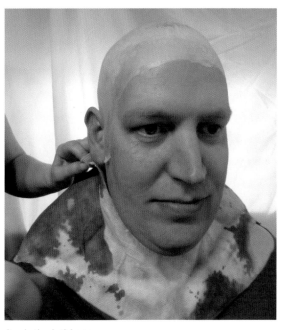

Apply the bald cap.

problems later in the day. It tends to get fuzzy with dirt, lint and whatever else might stick to it, causing a grubby line in the make-up.

At this point it's also a good idea to mark out the patches on the centaur's head so they line up with those on the face. An eyeliner pencil is used for this. These lines can be followed like a map when it comes to painting.

Step 2: Next mix up some PAX paint in the same brown as the main body. You will only need enough for the bald cap and to blend the edges on the appliance.

The best way to get the paint on quickly and effectively is to use a piece of sponge and dab it on. Build it up in a couple of layers until you have

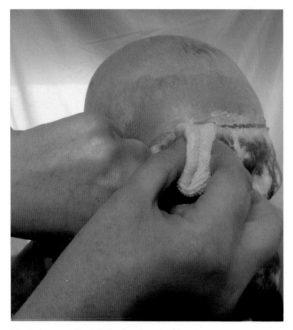

Mark the position of the forehead with talc.

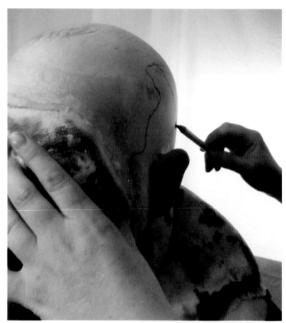

Draw patches with an eyeliner pencil.

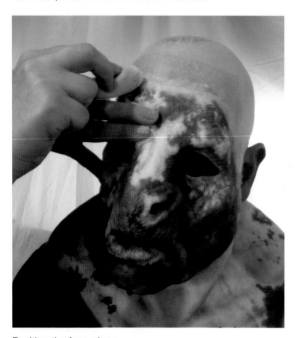

Position the face piece.

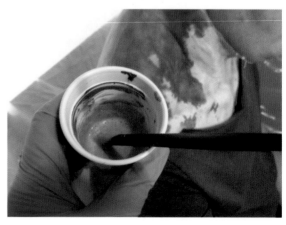

Mix up some brown PAX paint.

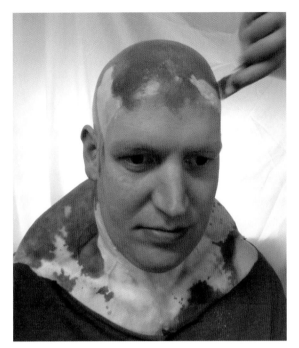

Colour the bald cap.

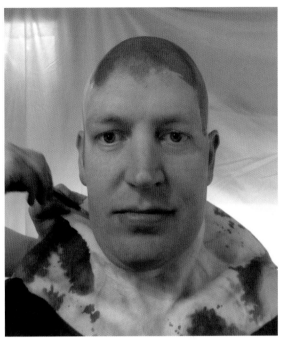

Starting to glue the neck piece in place.

a uniform colour on the cap. PAX is opaque, but if the actor has a lot of dark hair under the cap you can put down a layer of reddish orange first to cancel out the dark tone of the hair. You can then go ahead and apply the brown colour over the top.

Step 3: You can now start to glue down the neck. If you are doing this simply for a photo in a portfolio, you will only need to tack it down. If, however, it has to be worn for a performance where an actor or stunt performer has to wear it for twelve hours or more, then it would need to be really well secured.

With bigger pieces like this you can position the piece and then add a stripe of glue, usually in a central position such as the front and centre of the neck. This will ensure that it remains in position, while allowing you to manipulate the piece so that you can get underneath to add more glue.

For a piece such as this, make sure the areas close to the neck are secured. These need to

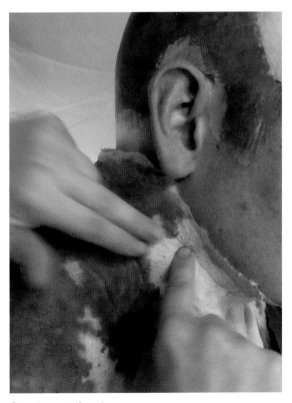

Glue the rest of neck.

Pull down to expose the edge.

If necessary use a bigger brush.

locked on for better movement. You may find an angled brush gives you better access here. You will also find that putting pressure on the fleshy part of the prosthetic directly underneath the edge creates a gap at the top that the glue brush can fit into.

When you've worked your way around the neck, you should flip up the bottom half and look at the area you are gluing. If it's large, use a bigger brush as it will reduce the time needed, and every little bit helps. Use large sweeping motions to get the glue on and then allow the piece to gently sit down onto it. Make sure the collarbone on the sculpt locks in nicely to the actor's own.

Step 4: Foam latex edges, unlike silicone and gelatin, will not dissolve with any medium, therefore you must use a spatula and the filler or Cabo-patch to fill in any edges or gaps. You can then stipple a layer of Pros-Aide cream over all the edges, including any areas you have filled, using a red stipple sponge. This type of sponge is great for edges as it has a subtle texture due to its small pores. The orange stipple sponge seen here has a larger cellular structure and will subsequently leave more texture behind. Remember you only need the tiniest piece as it will be disposed of afterwards, so don't waste it.

Fill the edges.

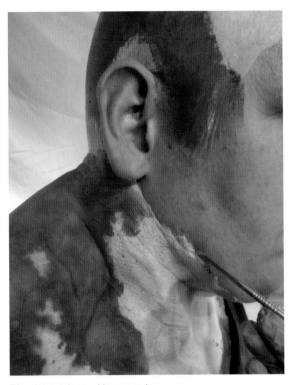

Blend the edges with a spatula.

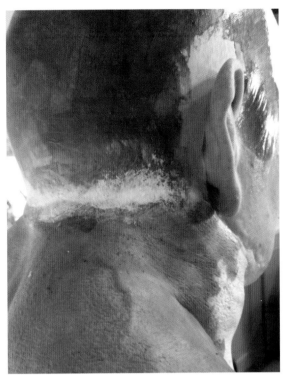

Blending the neck.

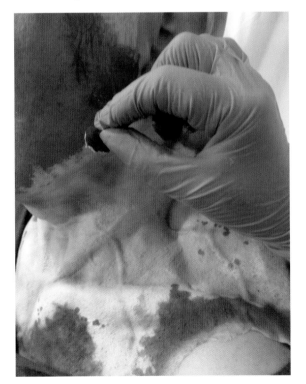

Stipple with a sponge to create texture.

You will find it is beneficial if you try to feather the line you create with Pros-Aide cream as this will blend the edge better. This time you can use a hairdryer to accelerate the drying time. It is best to have one with a cool button to give you more control over the air temperature. It's also good time management if you can work on something else within the make-up. This way you can leave the filled edges to dry by themselves, which is usually preferable to using a blow drier in someone's face. You will know when the cream is completely dry as it will have gone from a milky white colour to clear and shiny. You need to powder everywhere you have filled or put Pros-Aide stipple on using a no-colour powder and a powder puff. These powdered areas will later be coloured over to blend everything in and give the make-up a uniform appearance.

Step 5: It's time to glue the eyebrow hair. This is done to flatten the hair and also to direct hair away from the prosthetic edge. You don't want

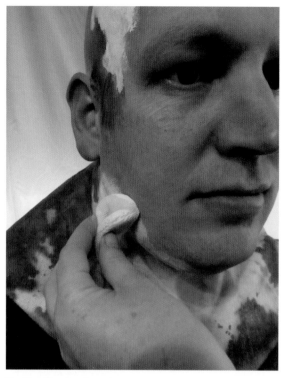

Powder the glued area.

stray eyebrow hairs to pop out from under the top edge of the eye area as it doesn't look good. You will also find that during the day the actor will get hot, resulting in perspiration on their forehead, be assured this sweat will look for an easy route out. If the eyebrow hairs are breaking the edge of the appliance, a mixture of glue and sweat will escape thorough the gap. Once this starts it will be difficult to stop and it's your job to maintain the make-up and mop this up – this is not pleasant for anyone involved! Prevention is definitely the best course of action.

With the safety of the performer in mind, hold a cotton round over the eye area. To further prevent potential glue drips, use a flat brush and don't load it with too much glue. You should only use neat glue in this area. Don't thin it as it makes it too runny and again it can drip. Always squeeze out any excess glue on the side of the glue cup or on a paper towel.

Don't forget to powder once the glue has dried.

Glue and flatten the eyebrows.

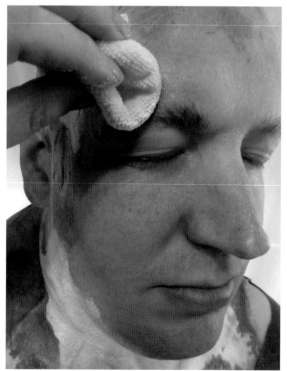

Powder the eyebrows.

Step 6: In order to help adhesion you can give the performer's face a cleanse with an astringent. This will remove any oils and help the glue stick better.

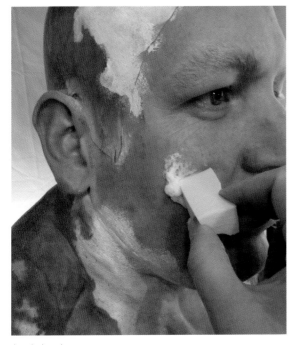

Use an astringent to cleanse the skin.

Apply barrier cream.

You may also want to use a barrier foam. Derma Shield is an industry standard as it doesn't affect the glue. There are probably other brands but this one is tried and tested and will help protect the performer's skin as well as aid the removal process.

Step 7: Place a thin line of glue down the centre of the performer's nose and also down the inside of the prosthetic nose. Position the two of these together. You can now flip back the sides of the

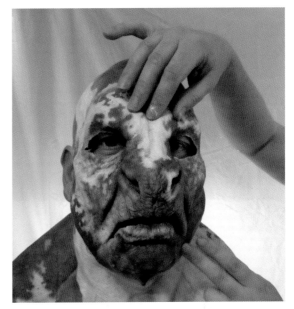

Tack the centre of the nose.

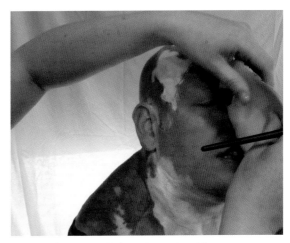

Run the glue outwards from the centre of the nose.

prosthetic to see where you are gluing. Continue working from the centre to the outside edge.

The placement of the nostril air holes on this prosthetic means that it's easier for the performer to breathe through his mouth.

When gluing the area around the eyes, aim for one good sweep of glue so that when you lay down the piece you don't need to go back in. The less you need to work around this area the

better. As the pieces are made from foam latex they have a certain amount of stretch to them, which is helpful when working with a generic piece. Just don't overstretch it as it will tear. You may also find you have to add padding to some areas if the piece is too big. This can be done with a little cotton pleat used as stuffing.

When the eye section is complete you will still be able to continue in a similar fashion around the rest of the face. This is a particularly good technique to use if you are using Pros-Aide glue as you can add the glue to the face and gradually position the piece. Here Telesis 5 glue is being used as it can easily be lifted and repositioned using the additional thinner. The glue is very expensive but a little goes a long way. There are other similar types and new additions appearing on the market all the time, so you will need to do your research, carefully reading the instructions as the application technique can vary. Pros-Aide is cheaper, but a little more unforgiving as it sticks fast on contact, although with care it may be possible to use IPA to re-lift the edges.

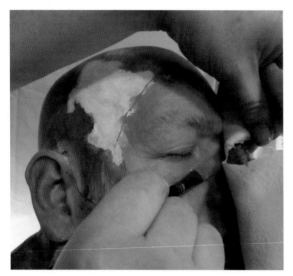

Gluing under the eye.

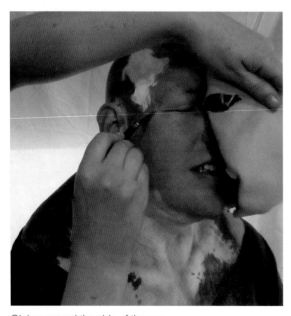

Gluing around the side of the eye.

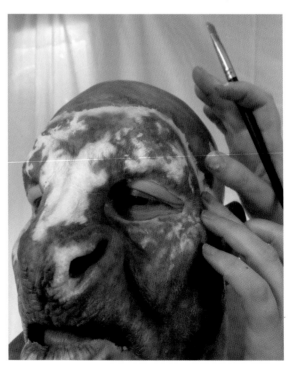

Position the piece into the glue.

Step 8: When gluing the area of the lips, pull down just below the mouth area. This will help position the mouth. Press the glued area down using a cotton tip.

Pros-Aide cream is useful when it comes to sealing the mouth area, which can be problematic as it moves a lot, it can get wet and the edges can lift up. Dry the inside of the lip area and have the performer open their mouth slightly so you can apply the Pros-Aide cream using a clean cotton tip. Make sure it is thoroughly dry and powder the area carefully before they fully close their mouth because otherwise it could stick.

If you need to work extensively around the mouth, wear gloves. Some artists wear gloves for an entire application, while others feel they hinder them. It's personal preference really. For working with PAX paint and cleaning off make-up gloves are essential, but you should be aware that they aren't always as hygienic as you might think. Your hands will sweat a lot when you wear

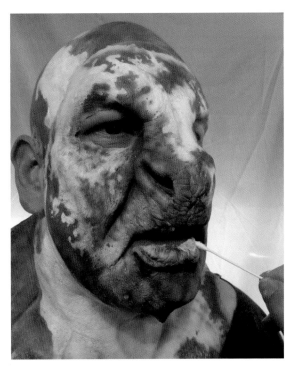

Seal around the mouth.

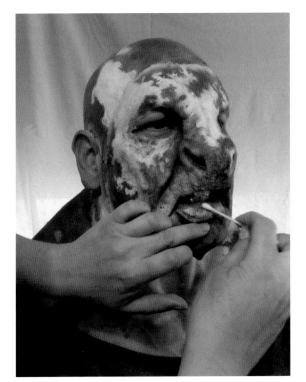

Pull down the mouth piece to apply the glue.

tight gloves for long periods of time, and this sweat can run down your wrist, which isn't nice for anyone. Remember when you take the gloves off you should thoroughly wash your hands, otherwise they may have an unpleasant odour from sweat, which is not so nice when you are working so close to someone's face. (The same applies if you are a smoker. Be aware of odours and invest in a hand sanitizer with essential oils.) If you find your hands start to get sticky from the glue you can have some alcohol wet wipes nearby. You can also add a little powder and rub it into your hands to help. Vinyl or nitrile gloves are preferable, as the smell of latex gloves can be a bit much for some performers, especially close to the face.

Step 9: This time the ears have been released from the bald cap as we are going to stick the new ears directly on top. You will need to position these with the help of a mirror to make sure they are level.

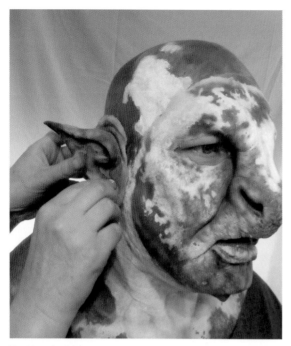

Position the ears.

The ears should be balanced when seen from the front.

Step 10: Now that everything has been glued into position and sealed, you can begin to camouflage the visible edges by painting them using a combination of the white and brown PAX as well as alcohol-activated inks.

Check the position of the ears in the mirror.

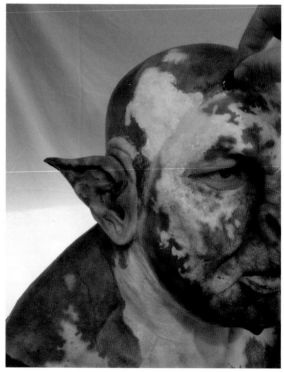

Blend the edge of the forehead.

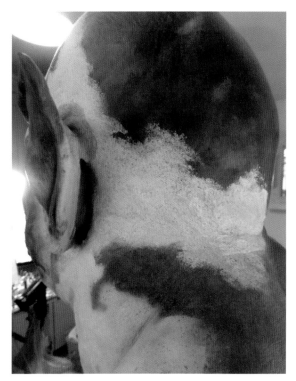

Stipple sponge on white PAX.

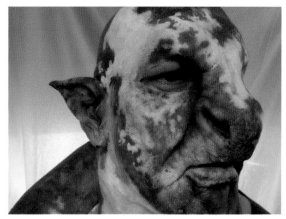

Blending the colours together.

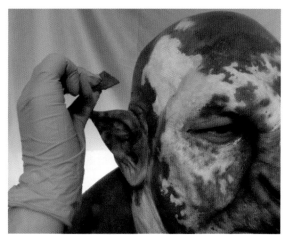

Stipple sponge on brown PAX.

TOP TIP

If you find that the eye area is popping a little at the sides, a micro flocked tip is useful. This will hold a small amount of glue and can be bent at an angle to enable you to reach tricky places.

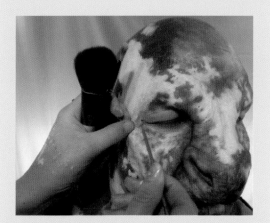

Fixing the area around the eye that hasn't adhered properly.

Step 11: The painting techniques implemented on this make-up include using the airbrush, as this was used for the initial pre-paint. The stencils will be used again to tie in the same patterns found on the areas already painted. When you are using an airbrush on a person's face, especially around the eyes and mouth, you need to turn the pressure down a little, as too much air can blow open the eye or mouth and be uncomfortable for the performer.

It is also a good idea to use a tissue or a cotton pad to cover the areas you don't want the paint or air to get into. For the comfort of the performer it is also useful to give them a small fan to help with the fumes.

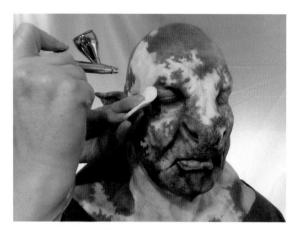

Use the airbrush to tie in the paint scheme.

Airbrushing through stencils.

It is a sign of consideration to the performer to wrap the cable of the airbrush around your arm as it keeps it away from their body. Be aware of their personal space and your equipment. It's also important to point out that you shouldn't lean your hand or body on the performer when doing a make-up. Of course it happens sometimes, as often the make-up artist is so engrossed in what they are doing they just aren't aware of it, but it's unprofessional.

The stencils will be used again to tie in the patterns found on the areas that are already painted. You will find that using these across the seams helps disguise them more.

When it comes to working around the ear you can gently place a cotton ball over the ear or ask the actor to do this themselves. You should always communicate with them, telling them where you are going to spray and let them know when you are changing from one side of the face to the other. They usually sit with their eyes closed to let you get on with your work, but sudden changes can startle them and they could open their eyes at the wrong moment, so be considerate. The more times they sit for make-up the more used they will get to the various stages.

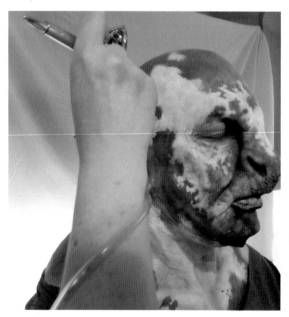

Wrap the cable around your wrist to keep it away from the performer.

Block the ear with a cotton ball.

Test the paint flow on a tissue.

Blending around the eyes with cremes and eye shadows.

Step 12: When you are happy with the progress you are making on the colouring, you may want to get into some finer detailing. If you are going to do some freehand airbrushing, hold a tissue next to the area you will be painting and do a practice spray on that before you commit yourself to the actual face. This helps you evaluate the flow of paint and how it will look. Airbrushes can be temperamental, so it's helpful to have a spare in case the first one clogs up and you haven't time to clean it.

Step 13: Don't use alcohol paints when you are blending the colour into the eye area. Instead you should opt for creams and eyeshadows as they are much kinder and safer.

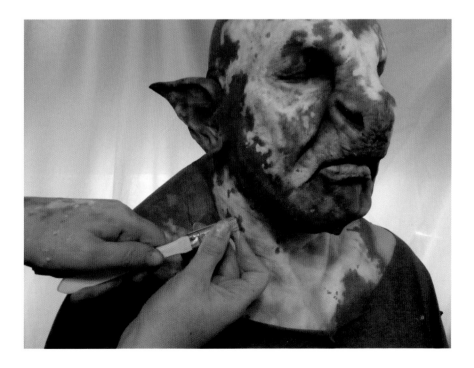

Using a chip brush to flick inks and create a spatter effect.

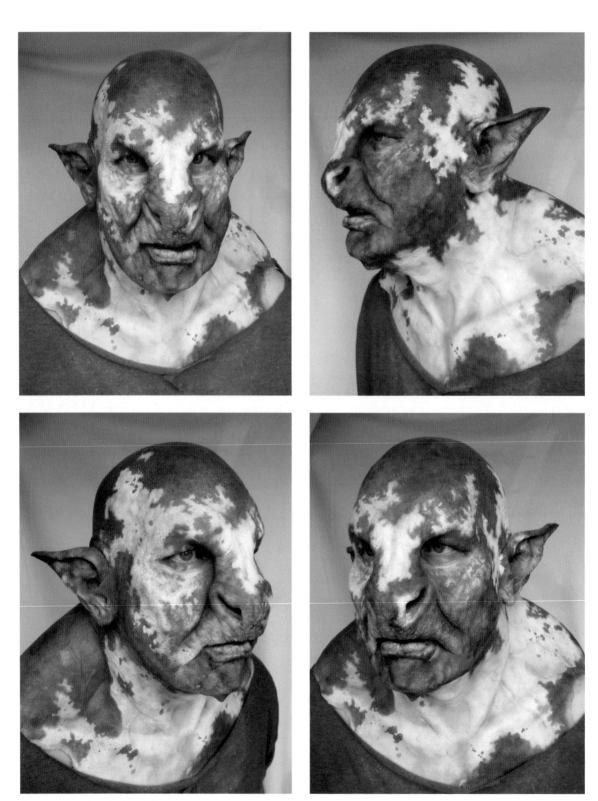

The completed and painted Centaur.

The final colouring stage is to use a cut-down chip brush to spatter some tones over the areas that need them. This ties everything together beautifully.

This ends the prosthetic application. As can be seen from the photos, the paint job has been blended all the way around the head, but the hair hasn't been added yet.

In order to show what your design will look like as a completed character you will need to add a hairpiece and some accessories. You can use Photoshop as a tool to show how it would look with the addition of creature eyes. For film or TV work, of course, these would be contact lenses, but it's important to remember that contact lenses must only be provided and inserted by a qualified lens technician. There are a few companies that deal with FX lenses for film and TV.

In this case the eyes have been Photoshopped in the final picture and the colouring has been changed to sepia, which gives more atmosphere to the character and also illustrates how a character make-up like this could be used in print.

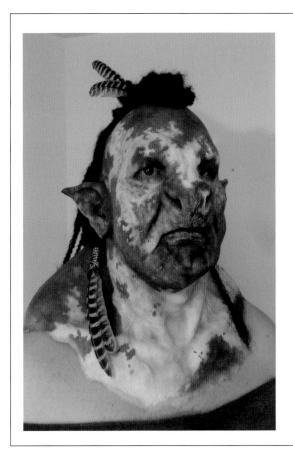

Complete and compare.

PART 4

LION CHARACTER: ADDING EMBELLISHMENTS AND SELF-APPLICATION

11

MAKING NOVELTY CHARACTER TEETH

In this part we are going to look at how you can embellish a character with the addition of custom-made prosthetic novelty dentures and hair. These elements can really change the look of a character and are worth considering if you want a more complete design.

We will be taking a generic foam latex appliance and turning it into a lion. When you have an animal character you should attempt to disguise as many human features as possible. This can be achieved by incorporating animalistic hair, as well as adding some authentic-looking animal teeth. These may be small details but it is always a good idea to push the boundaries of your design as far as possible.

Many prosthetic artists shy away from doing hair, while others embrace it. Sometimes when working as a professional you will find that a separate hairdresser will fit the wigs and hairpieces on your character, but you may have to do it yourself. In the following chapter you will learn a quick way to make an animal hairpiece and also how it can be blended into the hair on a facial prosthetic.

We will start, however, by describing how you can make a set of novelty teeth to further enhance your prosthetic creation and bring more realism to it.

Safety warning: When you need a set of custom teeth to enhance the design of a character in film or television production you would go to a professional company where a dental technician will make them for you.

If, on the other hand, you want to know how to make some teeth for yourself the techniques described below will set out a relatively quick way to do this. It must be stressed immediately, however, that these techniques only apply if you wish to make a set of wearable theatrical teeth appliances for yourself, but even then you do so at your own risk.

The purpose of this chapter is not to teach you dentistry. The following guides are only for the use of wearable theatrical teeth appliances. They are not to be worn every day, nor can you sleep with them. They are for novelty use only and you should never ingest food or drinks while wearing them. Neither should you engage in stunt work, running or any other activity while wearing them.

You should be aware that you run the risk of causing damage to teeth or tissue. *Do not* use this technique to make teeth if you have braces, caps or any other orthodontic addition attached. You could very easily do damage to things like fixed retainers, which could end up costing you a great deal of money and pain.

In the event that you feel discomfort while wearing theatrical teeth, contact your dentist immediately.

TEETH SUPPLIES

In order to make dental appliances you will need to use materials from a specialist dental supplier. You may also purchase everything you need from some make-up effects suppliers in the USA, but you should be aware that the UK has stricter laws and such items are more difficult to acquire.

This teeth kit is supplied by the US company The Monster Makers and comes with everything you need to make a couple of sets of fake teeth. Before you start you should read all the information that comes with the kit, which contains the following:

- 8oz dental alginate
- Complete dental tray set in 3 sizes

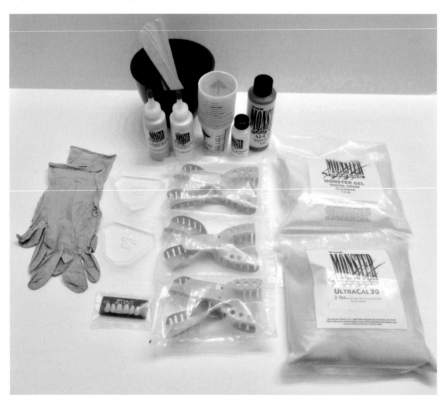

Equipment for casting teeth.

- 2lb UltraCal 30
- 2 base formers
- 3oz pink acrylic set
- 3oz tooth shade set
- 4oz Alcote separator
- 1 small rubber mixing bowl
- 6 tongue depressors
- 1 set pre-made upper anterior teeth

Please note that the following components, although part of the kit, were not used in this demonstration:

- 3oz pink acrylic set
- 1 set pre-made upper anterior teeth
- 4oz Alcote separator

CASTING TEETH

Taking teeth impressions

Just like any custom prosthetic appliance, you will need to take an impression of the area you wish to alter. In this case you need an impression of your teeth.

Step 1: You will need to use a tray that fits into your mouth and holds the alginate in place so you will be able to make the cast. Three trays of

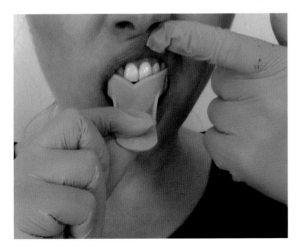
Select the dental tray that fits.

different sizes and shaped like a horseshoe are include in the kit. You need to choose the one that fits into your mouth with your own teeth positioned in the centre area and enough clearance around the edge, ensuring that you can fit your lip comfortably over the edge. The trays have a handle you can hold on to for ease. You should wear gloves for hygiene.

Step 2: When you have decided which tray to use, set it aside on a piece of kitchen towel and get ready to mix the alginate. This isn't ordinary alginate – it's dental alginate specifically designed for the purpose of making teeth impressions. It has a mint flavour and sets very quickly. *Never* use normal alginate to take teeth impressions.

For the dental alginate you need to mix one part powder to one part water. Remember the alginate rule: you need to add the water to the powder, not the other way around.

Weigh the alginate powder.

Mix the dental alginate.

Step 3: Next you can add the water and mix quickly and thoroughly with a tongue depressor or wooden mixing stick. You must work quickly as you are on a timed countdown as soon at the water hits the powder.

Step 4: Fill the top tray only with the alginate mix, spreading it and pushing it down well into the former. Try not to get any pockets of air trapped at this point or it will ruin the cast. Slightly overfill the tray towards the front.

Step 5: Carefully put the tray in your mouth. You will need to open wide and position it, then bite down into the middle of the alginate. You only get one chance to get this right, otherwise you will have to start again. You don't want your teeth too close to the edge as this will also mean a recast. There should be an even amount of material all around your teeth. Lean forward over a sink as you may drool a bit – definitely don't lean back as alginate can run down your throat. All in all it's not the most pleasant experience, and some people have a gag reflex. Just try to relax. It will be over quickly as the alginate sets fast.

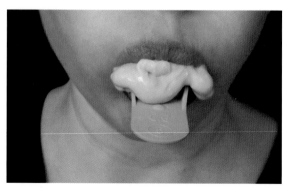

Place the filled tray in the mouth.

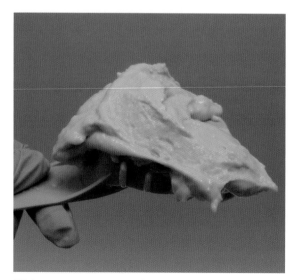

Fill the top tray with alginate.

Step 6: It's a good idea to keep a little of the alginate mix so you can see when it has set. This will indicate when it is safe to remove the tray. Again you should do this over a sink. You may have to gently wiggle the tray around to break the seal around your teeth.

Check to see if the mix has set.

Check the cast to make sure it's good. You can then leave it to soak in clean water while you repeat the process for the bottom teeth.

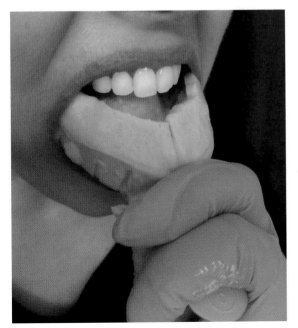

Remove the tray when the alginate has set.

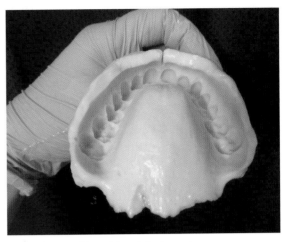

Check the condition of the alginate cast.

Soak the alginate cast in water until needed.

Step 7: Rinse and repeat! You should now have two negative moulds of your teeth. You need to transform these into positive moulds by filling them with plaster.

Plaster positives

Step 8: The plaster that comes with this kit is UltraCal 30, which is a grey plaster that dries to an extremely hard finish. You will usually need twice as much water as powder. This time put the water into a mixing bowl and add the powder

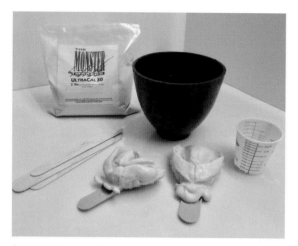

Second stage cast.

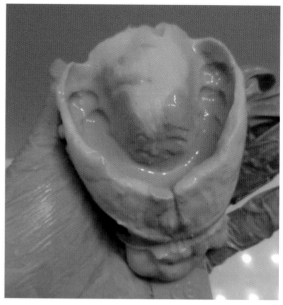

Fill the teeth cast with plaster.

to the water until the plaster starts to form little islands and eventually resembles a dry riverbed.

Make sure the plaster is really well mixed. By using your hands you will be able to feel when all the lumps have gone. You then need to paint in a fine layer on the teeth. This is the detail coat that ensures all the details are captured, and it also helps to eliminate air bubbles on the teeth surface.

Fill up the rest of the teeth mould and allow it to set.

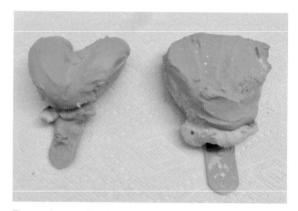

The teeth casts filled with plaster.

Mix the plaster.

Step 9: This particular kit also comes with little plastic former trays, which are very useful in providing a flat base for your teeth. These also need to be filled with plaster, so when the teeth moulds are set and have completed the chemical cycle of heating and cooling, which usually takes a few hours or is completed overnight, you can remove the alginate and plastic tray and dispose of them. Then repeat the process of mixing a smaller amount of plaster and filling the plastic former. Use warmer water to speed up the setting time of the plaster. When it has begun to set to a firm consistency, embed the teeth moulds down into it and leave to set.

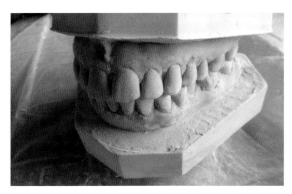

The pair of plaster sets.

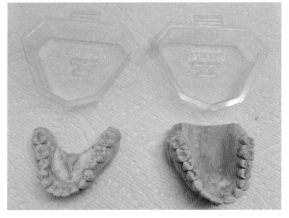

Making the plaster bases.

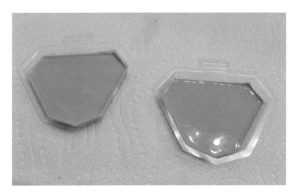

Fill the plastic tray.

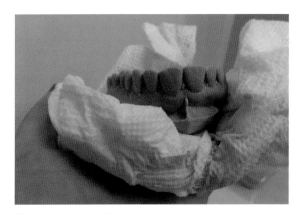

Finished plaster teeth cast.

The finished cast shows both sets of teeth mounted to the base. If you need to clean up the teeth cast this can be done when the plaster is freshly taken out of the mould, as it will not have fully set and will still be a little soft.

SCULPTING NOVELTY CHARACTER TEETH

Materials and tools

- Dental articulator (optional)
- Small files and rasps to clean up plaster teeth or a sharp knife
- Rasp tool
- Wet and dry sandpaper (this is a very fine grit black sandpaper that can be used wet or dry)
- Respirator mask
- Scales
- Silicone mould-making material – OOMOO is a good choice
- Large mixing bucket
- Mixing sticks
- Glue gun and glue sticks
- Oil-based clay – to sculpt new teeth
- Lighter fluid – to smooth the sculpt
- Water clay – to build walls
- Sculpting tools
- Vinyl gloves
- Vaseline

- Ultra 4 epoxy parfilm – mould release spray
- Mini kitchen/lighter torch
- Alcohol-activated palette inks
- Clear gloss coat – available from dental suppliers
- Dremel multitool and safety goggles

Necessary moulds

Now that you have your teeth in plaster form there are a couple more moulds you need to make before you can begin working on your new teeth. You need to make silicone moulds of the plaster teeth that will provide a negative master copy. This is an essential safety measure should anything happen to the plaster teeth. It would be time consuming and costly if you had to repeat the process.

Step 1: Hot glue the base of the plaster teeth – just one little blob in the centre is fine – to a

firm surface to keep them from moving around or rising to the top of the silicone mould. Cut the bottom of a large plastic cup and place it around the plaster teeth, making sure the teeth are in the centre of the cup and that there is enough clearance around the outside edge of the teeth (about ½in).

The cup then needs to be securely fixed to a surface using the glue gun, making sure there are no gaps or you risk the silicone leaking out. When the cup is secured, fill it with a tin-based silicone mould-making material such as Mold Max 30, OOMOO or Bluestar Bluesil V-1065 silicone. Remember to use the high pour technique in order to stretch out the air bubbles. OOMOO silicone is a good choice as there is less chance of air bubbles due to its consistency. You also don't need scales to mix it as it's a 1:1 mix. You can get away without using a release on the plaster teeth as the silicone won't stick to them, but for added security you could always apply a very thin coat of Vaseline.

Step 2: Leave the silicone mould to cure, preferably overnight. Depending on the type of silicone you are using the cure time may be faster. Read the instructions and data sheets to find out when

Hot glue a plastic cup around the teeth to make a mould.

Finished silicone teeth cup mould.

Plaster teeth in the mould.

it will be safe to remould. If you keep a little of the same mix you poured into the mould, you can test it to see if it has cured.

Step 3: When you remove the plaster teeth from the mould you might need to clean up the inner edges where a little silicone ran under the mould. This can be done with fine scissors.

Remove the plaster teeth.

Step 4: Next you need to give the new silicone teeth mould a thorough coating of Ultra 4 epoxy parfilm release spray. Don't let it pool up in the mould: two or three thin layers will provide good coverage, letting each dry for a few minutes.

Step 5: You now need to mix up a smaller batch of silicone, which will be poured into the silicone mould you have just made. Allow this to fully set.

Coat the silicone teeth mould with spray release.

Pour silicone into the new mould.

When everything has set, the silicone teeth can be removed from the silicone mould. You will now have your plaster teeth, a master silicone mould and a set of silicone rubber teeth.

Repeat this process with the bottom set of teeth.

Store the silicone negative teeth mould in a safe place so you can use it again if you need to make another set of teeth.

Finished moulds.

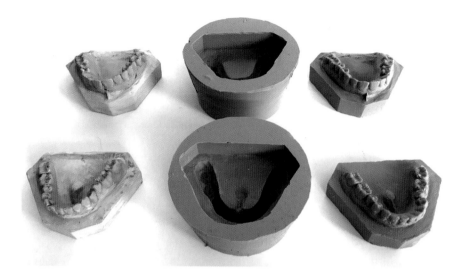

Upper and lower moulds.

Set the rubber teeth aside (you will need them in Step 8 below).

Take the plaster teeth and move on to the next stage.

Sculpting new teeth

Step 6: You are ready to start sculpting some new teeth. If you want your creature to have both upper and lower sets you will need to be aware of the bite, which is where your teeth naturally fit together. It's important to sculpt the new teeth to fit with this bite. A tool that will help you determine how the two sets fit together is known as a dental articulator. This metal device is hinged in the middle, allowing you to open and close the two plates. Examples can be found relatively inexpensively on auction sites such as eBay. They are handy little gadgets and will help improve the fit of your teeth.

You need to set the teeth together in the natural biting position and then mount them on the articulator using hot melt glue and a glue gun. This may look a little crude, but it serves the purpose of holding the plaster teeth in place. When you are finished, they can also be carefully removed.

Dental articulator.

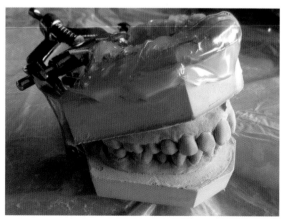

Glue the teeth to the articulator.

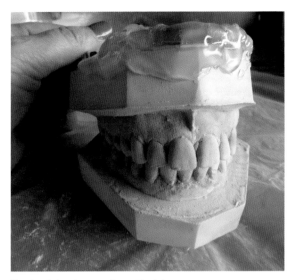

The teeth in place on the articulator.

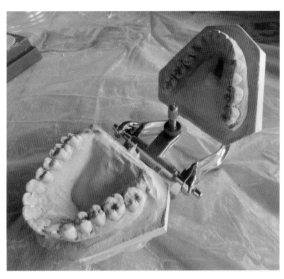

The articulator can hold the teeth open.

Now you need to find some reference pics to provide inspiration for the teeth. In this case the creature is a lion. Use the Internet and search through books with photos of lions with their mouths open. These photos of lion teeth were taken from a display at a local zoo.

In this case it is necessary to cover just the front eight teeth for the dental piece to stay in place without any sort of glue. The accuracy that can be achieved using the dental articular means that you can fit the overlapping teeth to your own bite. They will fit better in your mouth and should make speech clearer.

Look at the front view of the newly sculpted teeth and note how the sculpt doesn't go beyond the maxillary labial frenum. This is the little flap of skin that connects the inside of your upper lip to the gums just above the upper two front teeth. This is a delicate area and you don't want to damage this or the equivalent on the bottom gum. If you examine your own mouth you will notice there is quite a lot of space from the top of your teeth to the gum line where your gums end inside your mouth. Look at your own smile, see how much gum you naturally expose and match your sculpt to this.

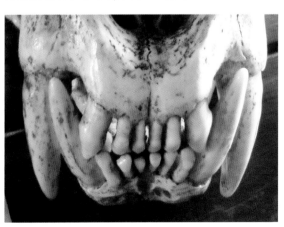

Reference material for lion teeth.

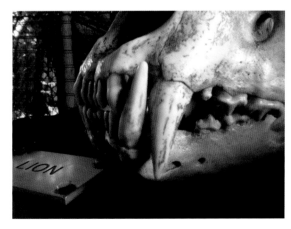

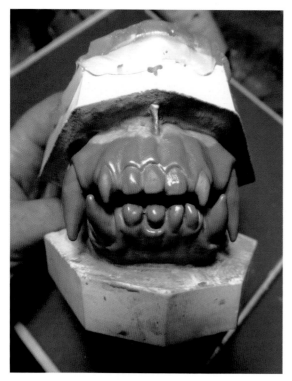

Front view of the sculpted teeth.

alter the shape of how your lip naturally sits over them. Make sure you smooth out the design with some lighter fluid or naphtha and a soft synthetic artist's brush, as you don't want your lips to catch on any rough edges.

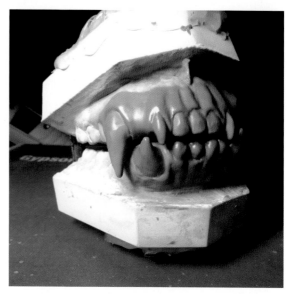

Three-quarters view of the sculpted teeth.

Also pay attention to how far up into your gums you place the sculpt. You will want these teeth to be comfortable to wear and you don't want to damage your teeth or any of the soft gum tissue.

Your new sculpted teeth will be bulky and will

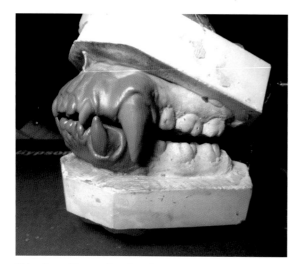

Side view of the sculpted teeth.

Top view of the sculpted teeth.

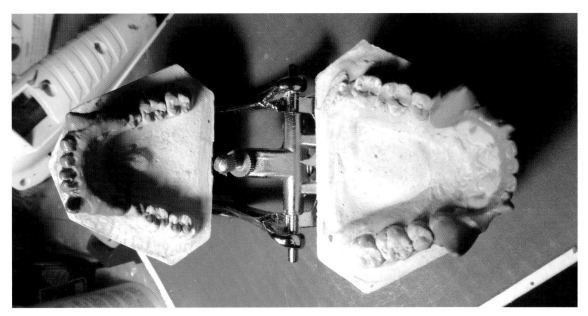

Teeth open.

Look at the placement of the back of the teeth when the articulator is opened up. The sculpt only slightly clips over the back teeth along the front. The pointed eye teeth should fit over your own ones. Again don't sculpt it so far up that it touches the gum area. This helps keep the new teeth more secure in your mouth.

When you are happy with your sculpt smooth it off with the lighter fluid and allow this to evaporate off. You can then mould it in the same way you did the original teeth. In order to do this you have to remove the teeth from the dental articulator *very carefully*. You don't want to ruin all your hard work at this point. It might help to reheat the glue using a small kitchen torch or a heat gun.

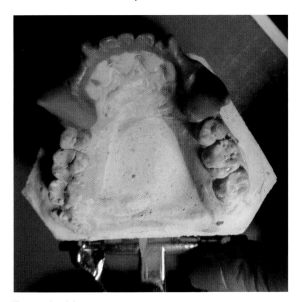

Top underside.

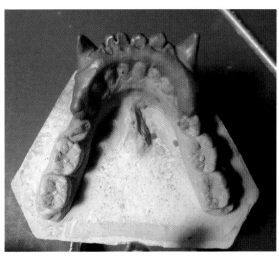

Bottom underside.

Teeth cup mould.

available at the time. It must be properly prepared before you can pour it into your mould. For this you will need scales, a large mixing vessel and a bigger mixing stick. Whatever type of moulding silicone you have you should always read the instructions. This particular silicone requires you to mix each component well before you combine them. You probably won't need as big a vessel as the one shown here, but this mix was intended

Large mixing bucket.

Step 7: You will need a little more silicone this time as it needs to cover all the new teeth.

You may find that using OOMOO silicone will make things easier as it's a 1:1 mix and you don't need to weigh it out on scales. Here, however, the silicone used was Mold Max 30 as that's what was

Some silicones will require scales.

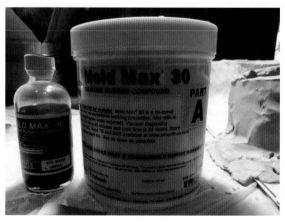

Silicone material.

Mix the silicone well.

Pink lion teeth mould.

for other mould projects at the same time. If you have a few moulds to run, mix a bigger batch. It's also worth pointing out that if you use a bigger vessel you can mix the product without it spilling over the edges.

The rest of the moulding process is the same as before, using the high pour method to stretch out any air bubbles that might appear in the mix. It can then be taken out of the mould according to the manufacturer's instructions.

Step 8: Remove the clay and plaster teeth from the mould once it has cured. You now have everything you need to make a set of new teeth. You will need the rubber teeth you made earlier (see Step 5). You are going to fill the Lion teeth mould you have just de-moulded with only the white (tooth) coloured acrylic and will be painting in the gum colour later. You will not need the pink gum coloured powder that also comes with the Monster Makers tooth kit. There are other ways that the pink acrylic powder can be used, but that would involve a more advanced demo. This particular demo is a fast, effective and easy way to make teeth.

The tooth acrylic that comes with the kit is a two-part powder (Polymer) and liquid (mono-mer). It's a self-curing acrylic system that sets to a very hard plastic when both elements are combined. It is going to be cast directly into the silicone mould.

You *must* be in a *well-ventilated* area while using this material and you should also wear a suitable respirator mask designed to deal with harmful chemicals of this kind.

There is no need to put a mould release on the silicone teeth moulds as the acrylic is easily release from them.

It's difficult to give exact measurements for the ratio of powder to liquid when making acrylic teeth as it depends on the application. Put the powder in a small cup such as a medicine cup (cups are provided with the kit) and then add the liquid monomer and stir until the consistency is like gravy.

The original rubber teeth in the new lion teeth mould.

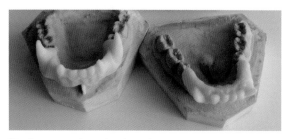

Newly cast teeth put back on the plaster teeth.

Step 9: Pour this liquid into the new teeth mould, tilting the mould forward a little to keep the acrylic towards the front. You will want to make sure this area is well coated as this contains the new teeth shape. (Don't worry about filling the back teeth, because you only need the first eight front teeth.) Pushing the material around with a sculpting tool or toothpick will help eliminate air bubbles. Make sure you have enough to fill the mould sufficiently.

Now take the rubber teeth and press them carefully into the mould. You may see some of the white liquid spill over the edge. This is fine as it simply means you have filled the area adequately.

Now you must wait for your mould to cure. It should be ready to de-mould in a couple of hours.

Step 10: When the mould is ready you can open it carefully. The acrylic will either stick to the rubber teeth or will remain in the mould. Carefully remove the new teeth. They might still be soft at this point, so handle them with care. Any excess material can usually be gently and carefully pulled off, although for larger repairs you might need to file or cut areas. If the acrylic has been left for some time it will have hardened more and you may need to use a Dremel tool to remove the excess.

If you find there are some holes in the acrylic teeth after you remove them from the moulds, dip a brush into the liquid monomer and then put the

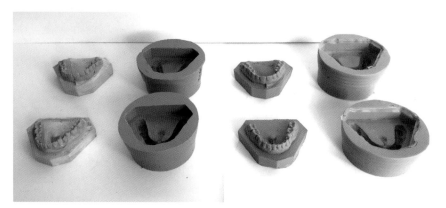

All the moulds needed to make novelty teeth.

wet tip into some powder polymer. This will soak up the powder, creating a little ball of acrylic that can be brushed over the hole, working it in to fill it up. Use more liquid to smooth it off. You may need to sand it smooth with some wet and dry sandpaper when it dries.

It's a good idea to put the new teeth back on the original plaster teeth. This will let you see how they fit and keep them more secure. You are now ready to paint the gums and teeth.

If you put all the moulds you need to make novelty teeth alongside one another you will notice that you can use the same silicone for all the components. The various colours that can be seen in the photo here are just because it was easier for this demo to show you the different moulds in different colours. Now let's paint!

PAINTING NOVELTY CHARACTER TEETH

Materials and tools

- Unpainted teeth

Teeth painting materials.

- Paintbrushes
- IPA – Isopropyl alcohol (99%)
- Alcohol-activated ink palettes
- Small cup for IPA
- Minute Stain clean liquid and glaze or equivalent gloss seal

Painting teeth

Once you have gathered your materials you are ready to put the finishing touches on the teeth. Keep the unpainted teeth attached to the plaster teeth former as this will make it easier to paint them.

Start by painting the gum colour with the alcohol-activated inks, using washes of colour and building it up gradually. A way to help make the gum look more fleshy is to leave lighter colours in the middle, as can be seen in the front and side views here. This technique helps make an opaque item look more translucent. You should also add some colour to the teeth close to the gum line. This will give them a more lived-in look and will add dimension.

Don't forget to paint the back of the teeth, too. You never know if they will show, particularly on the bottom set.

You could leave the teeth like this and then finish them with a glaze to seal them and give them a wet look. Animal gums, however, aren't always pink. Some have a few variations, so to add more interest a mottling effect has been added to the paint scheme on the gums.

The great thing about painting teeth using this technique is the ability to go back if you don't like something. Providing you haven't sealed the

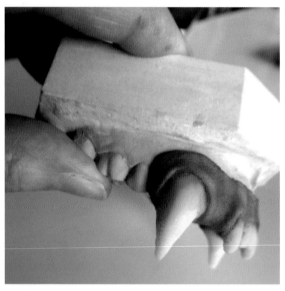

Side view of the painted gums.

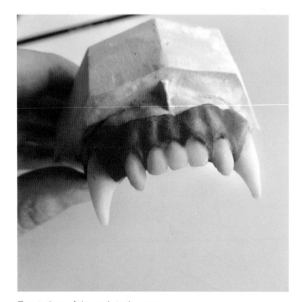

Front view of the painted gums.

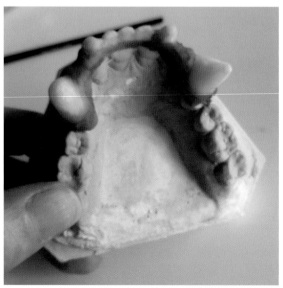

Inside view of the paint gums.

teeth with a gloss sealer, you can simply wipe off the paint with IPA and start over until you are happy with the paint job.

When you finally come to add the gloss coat to your teeth they will look even more realistic as they will appear wet, just like the teeth inside the mouth of a living creature.

As previously stated, there are other ways to make teeth and to colour them. Professional tooth colours called Minute Stains are quite expensive, so instead you can use the alcohol-activated palettes and then seal them with a gloss coat. Some people have been known to seal the teeth using a clear acrylic nail polish and letting it dry thoroughly. This will provide the desired sheen but is best reserved for teeth intended for a mask or creature sculpts. Professional gloss sealers are available from dental suppliers.

Now we have a set of dentures to enhance our prosthetic character!

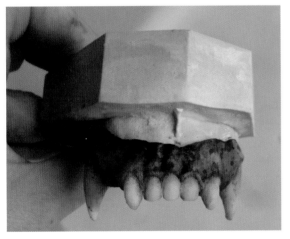

Paint mottling on the gums for more interest.

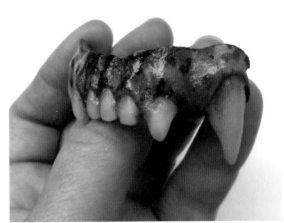

Glossy teeth.

12

FANTASY ANIMAL HAIR WORK

We have previously learned how to put hair on a realistic character (see Chapter 7). We will now look at hair work on a more fantastical animal or hybrid creature. This time it's going to be a self-application. As an FX artist it's a good idea to know what you are putting a performer through, so what better way than to experience it all yourself. Another advantage is that when you are starting out you will always have a model available.

These generic appliances really are a lot of fun and a good way to come up with a different interpretation of someone else's sculpt. I'm sure it's pretty interesting for the sculptors themselves to see what others come up with. The freedom of creativity is something artists strive for. We are going to look at how you can take an appliance like this and other elements that will make it unique – essentially hair and teeth. These can really change a character and make it look more interesting. Wigs and teeth can be bought online, but custom making something means you have more control and it will usually look better.

HAIR WORK

First let's see how to go about working some hair into this character, noting that lions are pretty much defined by a glorious mane. This particular piece will be a bit of a challenge since the forehead is fairly short. So how are we to tie the mane into the rest of the face piece without covering the whole thing in hair?

First we need to make a hairpiece and figure out how to blend it later.

Materials and tools

- Hair – a mixture of synthetic and real hair (purchased online)
- Tape measure
- Polystyrene head block
- Sharpie
- Pins – ball-headed pins are easier to see
- Wig cap
- Toothbrush – to brush hair
- Pros-Aide cream adhesive
- Comb
- Cotton tips
- Hair scissors
- Small pointed scissors
- Curved needle
- Strong thread
- Strong-hold hairspray
- Hair tongs
- Hair tong oven or gas kitchen lighter (if you don't have an oven)
- Plastic wrap, clear sticky tape, cotton pleat (optional) – only needed if you need to make the head bigger

Hair.

Getting started

The first thing you need to do is measure the circumference of the head on which this hairpiece is going. Luckily the head measurements were the same as the polystyrene head in this case, but if you find that the head measurements

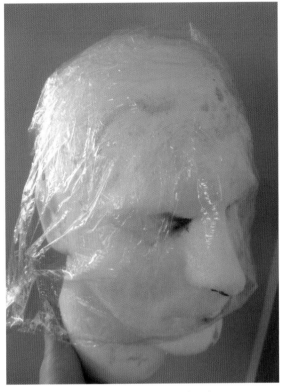

Adding plastic wrap to the polystyrene head.

are larger, take the poly head and pad it out with cotton wool, cling film and clear sticky tape until the desired circumference is achieved.

As a precaution plastic wrap was placed over the polystyrene head as it was uncertain whether glue would be needed to secure the hair to the wig cap. The plastic would then act as a barrier preventing the cap from sticking to the poly head. Secure the plastic wrap tightly with clear plastic tape.

Roll the stocking cap onto the polystyrene head and pin it to keep it in position.

Fold over the top of the stocking cap and pin it in place. You will need to put a few stitches into the corners to hold it in place.

This particular piece of fur fabric has the added bonus of having a stretchy backing. If you use normal fur fabric, however, you might have to sew it on in sections to allow it to stretch. Using zigzag stitches will also allow more stretch.

Polystyrene head.

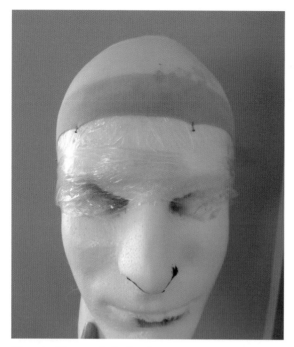

Pin a stocking cap to the head.

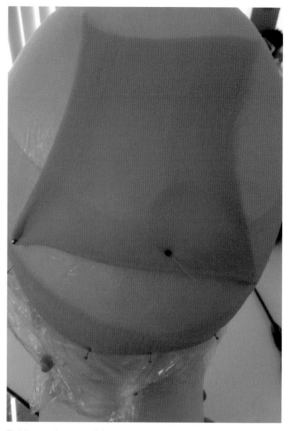

Fold over the top of the cap and stitch it in place.

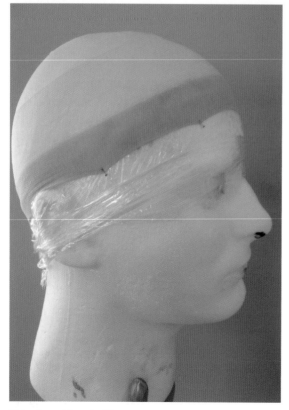

Side view of the stocking cap.

The design of the lion's mane will go into a point in the front of the forehead, much like a widow's peak. Pin the hair in the shape you want it to go, thread the curved needle and begin to sew it in place. Note the direction of the stitching. Try to follow around the shape of the hairline as best you can, manipulating the shape as you go until you achieve the desired design. Use the pins to help you.

Complete both sides of the face so that you have a symmetrical shape. You can then tack the rest of the fur fabric at intervals along the edge of the cap. It will be helpful at this point to pin the face on the head so you can see how it all looks.

Keep looking at your hairpiece from all angles, altering and tweaking it as you go.

Now that you have settled on the shape of the hair shape you will need to blend the face into the

Pinning and sewing the
fur fabric.

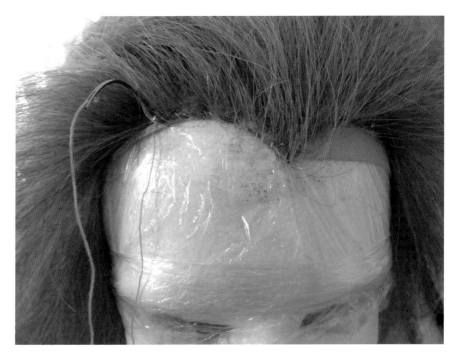

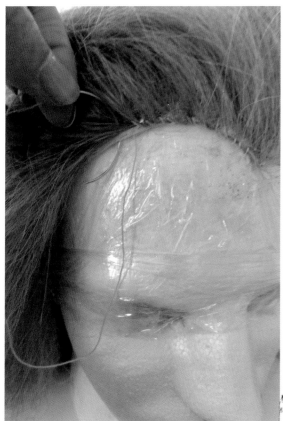

Using a curved needle.

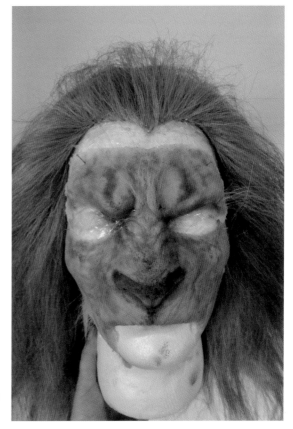

See how everything fits with the prosthetic.

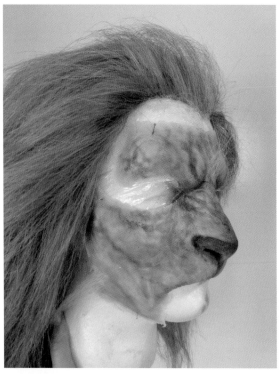

Side view of the prosthetic face with hair.

mane. This is done by hand-laying the hair in the same fashion as the gelatine Goblin (see Chapter 7). Pros-Aide cream is the glue of choice for this purpose as the hair will stick better.

Build the hair up in layers, paying close attention to the direction you lay it down as you will want it all to sweep back into the mane. In order to make this character more interesting he has been given a fantastical moustache and eyebrows. He resembles a jolly, whimsical sort of fellow and this is reflected in the design. You can wet the hair, apply hairspray and position it as you wish. Pin it into place and leave it to dry. The hair around the mouth and eyebrows is made of goat hair, which can be styled with heated tongs. Do *not* use tongs on synthetic hair as it will melt.

Your goal is to blend the eyebrow area into the widow's peak at the top of the head. Even though this is a fantasy character you want each element to look as realistic as possible

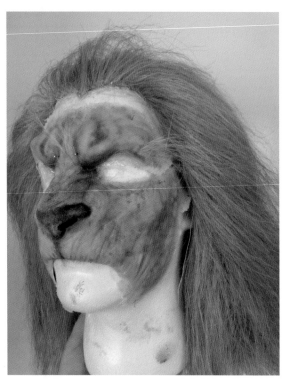

Three-quarters view.

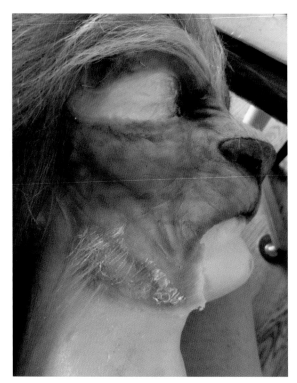

Hand-lay hair to blend it into the face piece.

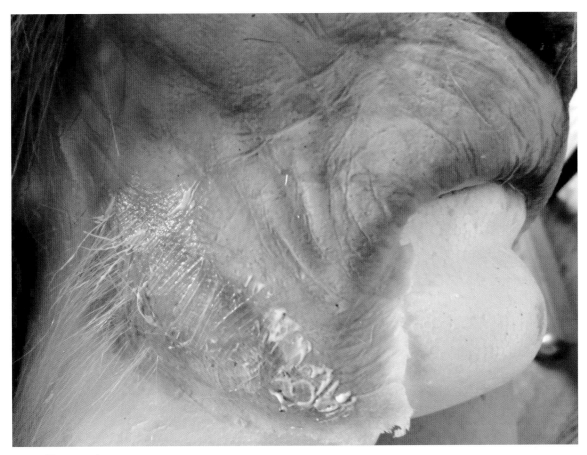

ABOVE: Close-up of
hand-laying.

Pin the hair into place
and set with hairspray.

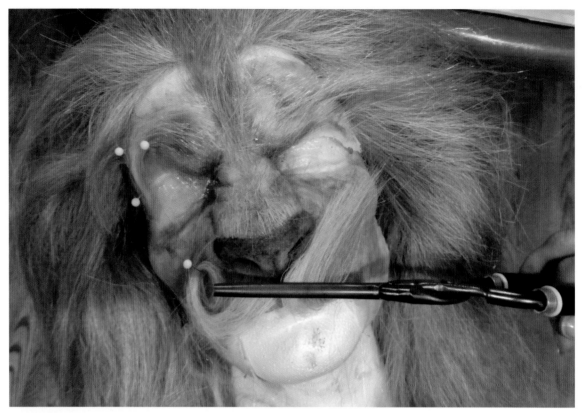

Tonging the hair.

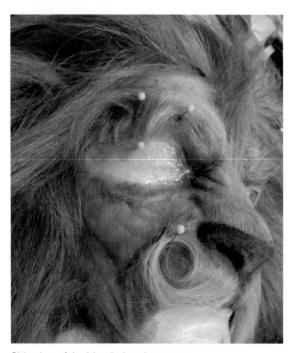

Side view of the blended eyebrow area.

SELF-APPLICATION

This final make-up is a self-application, which is a valuable exercise for any prosthetic make-up artist; it will help you understand how the process feels during application, wear and removal.

It will help you recognize how to improve on certain elements, what feels comfortable and what doesn't. Ultimately you will be able to relate to the person you are transforming.

Believe me, you will a better artist for it and gain more respect for performers and the hours they endure during this process, not to mention the effort that goes into their performances when they are wearing the appliances.

The demo illustrated here is a pre-made foam latex RBFX appliance painted using PAX, a 1:1 mixture of Pros-Aide adhesive and acrylic paint (see Chapter 10). It was chosen to provide a canvas to help show how the addition of teeth

Painting equipment.

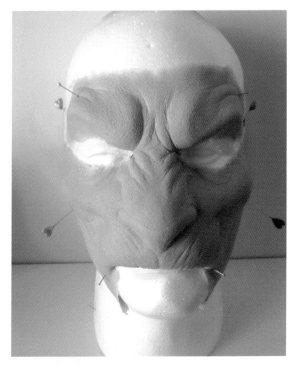

The unpainted lion.

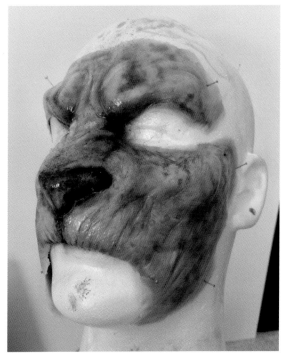

The painted lion.

and hair can take a prosthetic character to the next level of transformation. The views here show how it appeared in its raw unpainted state and after it has been painted.

Consider your design

This prosthetic character piece consists of only a small facial appliance; no chin appliance was included, so the hair was all hand-glued and applied directly to the skin using Pros-Aide cream to create the illusion of a beard. If this were a reoccurring character in a real production the hand-laid beard would have to be applied every day the performer plays. This is where you need to factor in time and budget, and come up with a

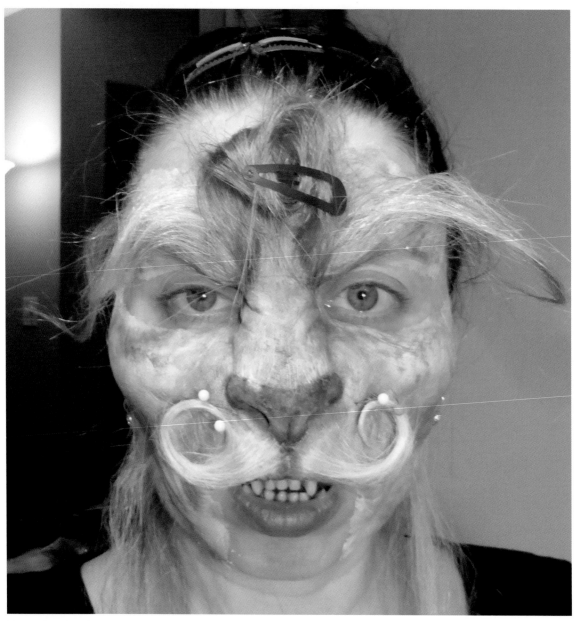

Lion self-application.

suitable solution. You may decide it's a lot easier to have a hair-punched chin piece that could be carefully removed and reused. This is a common practice on professional jobs. You could get a few applications out of a piece but the edges will suffer. With a design like this, however, you could simply lay more hair over the edge to hide the edges.

The dynamic of teeth

Another useful tip when applying a make-up involving novelty teeth is to have the performer wear the teeth when you apply the prosthetic. Novelty teeth invariably alter the shape of the mouth slightly, which makes sense as they are added on top of the performer's own teeth. Therefore it's beneficial to have the performer wear them when you apply the prosthetic to allow for the change in shape to their mouth. Otherwise it can put a strain on the appliance around the mouth area. You will want the performer to be able to speak and convey emotion freely and not feel restricted.

The more experience you have with prosthetics you will find that the mouth is the area that needs the most attention throughout a day's filming as it's the area that moves the most.

Some artists who devise character designs that include prosthetic dentures will even go as far as to make the teeth first so that the performer can wear them during the life casting process. This will give a sculptor a better representation of how the face is altered when the teeth are applied. The final creature will look more cohesive and the teeth will look like a natural part of the face, rather than jutting out from distorted lips that don't quite cover them. These are all things that must be considered during the design process of any character.

Applying a prosthetic with hair

If your appliance has a lot of hair, pin it out of the way to allow you to work freely. You will need to

prep the performer's hair in order to achieve a secure foundation to attach the hairpiece.

Slick the performer's hair back and add clips or elastic bands to give you something to pin the hairpiece or wig to. Place a wig cap over this. It will help keep the hair in place, since stray hairs can often escape as the performer heats up.

If a performer is very active in their role or doing stunt work, you will need to make sure the hairpiece or wig is especially secure. You can sew the hairpiece through the elastic bands, which should ensure it stays in place.

Many of the techniques used to bring this character to life are taken from various lessons throughout the book. The techniques shown can be mixed and matched to come up with your own unique design – the more original you can be the better.

The lion's mane.

The completed lion look.

CONCLUSION: BECOMING A PROFESSIONAL MAKE-UP ARTIST

Now that you have gained some insight into what is involved in the career of a professional prosthetic make-up artist, you may be wondering how to go about beginning a career in this field. This final chapter offers some tips as to how you could potentially go about this.

WHERE TO START

If you are wondering how you might learn more about this craft there are several ways you can educate yourself. Some of the many courses available are online and allow you to pick and choose the classes most relevant to you. This can be a cost-effective way to learn. There are also many schools that offer long and short term courses. A lot of them tend to be fairly pricey, so it's important to do your research before parting with any money. While there are some excellent courses out there, there are also a few that might not fully prepare you for work after you complete them. The best advice is to determine what you hope to gain from the course and to analyse exactly what the course can offer you. Some points to consider are as follows:

- What are the facilities like? Visit the school if you can.
- Who is the course taught by? Are they working professionals? What is their experience and reputation?
- What size are the classes? If they are large you won't get much one-to-one attention.
- Are the techniques taught up to date or are they dated? Look at the materials they use.
- Is the school connected or affiliated to a professional workshop? Many of them are and as a result they are more likely to teach current techniques. There may also be opportunities to gain work experience in the workshop.
- How long is the course? Do they offer support and career guidance afterwards?

Some students leave make-up school confident that the certificate they have obtained is enough to get them work. Often, however, it isn't. It's worth considering that you will be leaving the course with a lot of other people who have learned the same techniques, and there is the risk that the pictures in your portfolio might not differ much from those of your classmates. You need to take the techniques you've learned and apply them to your own personal projects in order to stand out.

If you are lucky to land a job you will most likely start out as a trainee This is where the learning will really begin.

OTHER WAYS TO LEARN

There are lots of books on the topic of make-up and prosthetics, as well as magazine publications specifically aimed at the craft.

Many prosthetic suppliers have online tutorials showing step-by-step demonstrations of how to use their products. They also sell some of their supplies in kits, which is useful when you first start out as they tend to be more affordable and they take the guesswork out of how much you will need. There are also DVDs and online videos, but you should be careful with online tutorials as many of them don't teach safe practices. Always make sure you are learning the correct way to do something. Do your research.

PHOTOGRAPHY AND THE IMPORTANCE OF A GOOD PORTFOLIO

It cannot be stressed enough that you need to photograph your work. You should make it a habit. It is the most effective way not only to showcase your ability but also to record your growth and progression. When you network regularly with prospective employers they can see how you've developed and progressed as an artist. They may be more likely to hire you as they will see the ability and passion you have as your work gets better.

When you are starting out you will need to compile a selection of your best work to show to prospective employers. What we do in this profession is very visual and there are more artists out there than there are jobs. It's extremely important that you start to think about how you can stand out from the crowd and gain positive attention about your work.

The best approach is to select three or four good quality pictures of your work. Be critical and only present your best handiwork. Prospective employers are busy and can tell from the first few photos if you are what they are looking for. They won't be interested in ploughing through pages upon pages of images. Also try to show a variety of techniques. If you choose three images, for example, make one a fantasy piece such as a

creature, one a realistic make-up, such as an old age piece, and a third of your choosing. Don't make the mistake of filling your portfolio with lots of blood and gore. If you include examples of casualty effects in your book, show the wounds cleanly painted with before and after shots of the blood added. Blood is often used to hide bad edges and it can be difficult to see the actual sculpt and colouring of the prosthetic. It is also the case that blood and guts are often simple to do and a prosthetic designer or workshop owner will want to see a variety of techniques.

This book shows you how to achieve a few different skills and implement them into a completed character. This is a useful method to show a variety of skills in a limited number of pictures.

Please only use photos of work that you actually did in your portfolio. If you worked on a group piece, clearly state the part you were involved in and always credit the other people who contributed to the final piece. Never try to pass off someone else's work as your own. Unfortunately people have tried to get away with stealing other artists' work, but the world of prosthetic artistry is relatively small even on a worldwide scale, so be assured you will get found out.

RÉSUMÉ

If you have managed to get some work experience, put it into a résumé. Make it clear and concise and easy to skim read. You should also include some pictures of your work with the résumé, but make sure the files are not too big. You may want to think about sending a link to a website or online file that contains images of your work. It's a true saying that 'an image is worth a thousand words'.

NETWORKING

Networking is crucial in this industry. If you are

serious about a career as a professional prosthetic artist you need to get to know people, especially those who might be future employers. It may seem overwhelming at first but there are many ways you can interact with working professionals.

The Internet has indeed made the world a much smaller and more accessible place. Many artists and prosthetic workshops have online photo accounts and personal webpages. You can follow their work online and they in turn can see yours.

You can also use the Internet to stay informed about upcoming make-up artist trade shows. These are events held specifically for the profession and are the ideal opportunity to actually get to meet other artists and employers face to face, chat to them and show them your portfolio.

You need to make an effort. It's about putting yourself in the right place at the right time. Nothing may come of your efforts at first, but keep working on your own personal projects, get involved with student films and keep doing as much as you can. This will eventually get noticed and you may be given an opportunity to work.

When this opportunity arises, use it wisely. Show up on time, be prepared, be helpful and learn as much as you can. Perhaps one of the most important things this book can teach you is that talent will get you noticed, but more importantly your attitude and personality will be noted. Since you will be working as part of a team you need to fit in with everyone. The most talented person in the world won't get employed very much if their attitude stinks. Make your first impression a good one.

CONCLUSION

Whether you are interested in the design and manufacture of prosthetic appliances or working as an application artist on set, remember that each person in their respective department is highly skilled. Don't get disheartened when you are starting out. Go easy on yourself and don't expect to be brilliant at everything right away. The old adage of practice makes perfect stands true.

Many professionals in this industry tend to focus on individual areas of expertise. They then become brilliant at that particular job, perhaps concentrating on sculpting, or they like painting or prefer mould-making.

When starting out you will want to showcase your skills. This will involve knowing a little about each stage in order to create an appliance or a creature. That may seem a little daunting but it's worth seeing your very own creation come to life on a performer's face.

Whether as a hobbyist, professional or aspiring professional, I hope this book has inspired you in some way to create your own prosthetic make-ups.

SUPPLIERS

Australia

Adelaide Moulding and Casting Supplies
Compressors, sculpting, moulding and dental
suppliers
www.amcsupplies.com.au

Barnes Products
Sculpting and casting suppliers
www.barnes.com.au

The Make-up Foundation
Make-up and SFX make-up suppliers
https://themakeupfoundation.com.au

Scotty's Make-up & Beauty
https://scottysmakeup.com.au

Canada

The Face Station
www.cmucollege.com/the-face-station

Sculpture Supply Canada (SSC)
www.sculpturesupply.com

Skycon Building Products
Mould-making and casting suppliers
www.skycon.ca

Studio F/X
www.studiofx.ca

Ireland

RPM Supplies
Sculpting, mould-making, FX make-up
suppliers
https://rpmsupplies.com

New Zealand

BODYFX New Zealand
Make-up and effects make-up suppliers
https://bodyfxshop.com

Makeup Collective
Make-up and SFX make-up suppliers
www.makeupcollective.co.nz

Sculpture and Modelling Supplies Ltd (SAMS)
https://www.sculpturesupplies.co.nz

Northern Ireland

MB Fibreglass
Casting, sculpting, mould-making suppliers
www.mbfg.co.uk

Scarva Pottery Supplies
Pottery, casting, sculpting, mould-making
suppliers
www.scarva.com

United Kingdom

Banbury Postiche Limited
Wig and hair supplies and tools
www.banburypostiche.co.uk

Crownbrush
Make-up brushes
https://crownbrush.co.uk

Guru Makeup Emporium
Make-up and SFX make-up suppliers
www.gurumakeupemporium.com

Mouldlife
Casting, sculpting, mould-making and FX
make-up suppliers
www.mouldlife.net

Neill's Materials
Casting, sculpting, mould-making and FX
make-up
www.neillsmaterials.co.uk

Pak Cosmetics
Hair weft, extensions, wigs, hair and make-up
supplies
www.pakcosmetics.com

Precious About Make-up (PAM)
Make-up and SFX make-up suppliers
https://preciousaboutmakeup.com

PS Composites
www.ps-composites.com

TILT Professional Makeup
https://tiltmakeup.com

Alec Tiranti Ltd
Casting, sculpting and mould-making
https://tiranti.co.uk

United States

Brick in the Yard Mold Supply
Casting, sculpting, mould-making and FX
make-up suppliers
www.brickintheyard.com

Crownbrush
Make-up brushes
https://crownbrush.com

Davis Dental Supply
Dental casting and mould-making supplies
www.davisdentalsupply.com

Frends Beauty
Make-up, hair and SFX suppliers
www.frendsbeauty.com

Hairymann's Closet
Overrun, clearance, and remnant fur fabrics
from National Fiber Technology
https://hairymannscloset.com

His & Her Hair Goods Co.
Hair weft, tools, wigs and wig supplies
www.hisandher.com

Laguna Clay
Sculpting materials
www.lagunaclay.com

Mohairwig
Animal and synthetic hair and wig supplies
http://shop.mohairwig.com

The Monster Makers
Casting, sculpting, mould-making and FX
make-up
www.monstermakers.com

Motion Picture F/X Company
Casting, sculpting, mould-making, FX make-up,
dental and pre-made prosthetic supplies
https://motionpicturefx.com

Naimie's Beauty Center
Make-up and FX make-up supplies
www.naimies.com

National Fiber Technology
Stretch synthetic fur fabrics
www.nftech.com

Nigel Beauty
Make-up, hair and special FX suppliers
www.nigelbeauty.com

Pearson Dental Supply
Dental casting and mould-making supplies
www.pearsondental.com

RBFX Studio
Pre-made foam latex and silicone appliances
https://rbfxstudio.com

Smooth-On Inc
www.smooth-on.com

Stage & Screen FX
www.stageandscreenfx.com

GLOSSARY

Acetone
Harsh and flammable chemical used to dissolve cap plastic edges.
Available at drug stores/chemists

Acrylic paint
When mixed with Pros-Aide adhesive this forms a stretchy durable PAX paint. PAX is mostly used on foam latex appliances. It can also be put directly on hairless skin.
Available at art supplies stores

Alginate
Powder made from derivatives of seaweed. When mixed with water it creates an impression medium used in life casting to capture the impression of a face or body.
Available at make-up FX stores and casting suppliers

Algi Slow
A retarder by DZ Models that allows newly mixed alginate to stick to cured alginate.
Available at make-up FX and casting suppliers

Artist's spatula
Metal or plastic flexible tool used to mix colours. Also used with prosthetic filler to smooth the edges of prosthetics.
Available from art supplies stores and make-up suppliers

Bald cap
Vinyl or latex cap that covers the entire head and hair, giving a bald appearance. Used to protect the hair during life casting or prosthetic application.
Available at make-up FX suppliers

Beading needle
Fine needle that makes a fine hair-punching tool when the top is cut at an angle.
Available at haberdashery and craft stores

Burlap
Coarse jute fabric used to reinforce moulds.
Available at haberdashery stores and casting and mould-making suppliers

Cabo-patch/filler

Pros-Aide cream with added fumed silica to thicken it to a paste. Used to patch prosthetics and repair edges to help them blend seamlessly into the skin. It can be bought or made. Wear a dust mask when working with fumed silica.
Available from specialist make-up suppliers

Chalk pen

Powder-filled pen that dispenses the powder via a toothed wheel to make easily removable lines on appliances.
Available from haberdashery and craft suppliers

Chavant clay

Oil-based plasteline clay used to make maquettes and prosthetics. Comes in a range of hardnesses.
Available from sculpting supply and make-up effects stores

Chip brush

Cheap wooden-handled brush with coarse bristles.
Available in hardware stores and from mould-making suppliers

Clay extruder

Metal tubular tool that allows you to press long spaghetti shapes of clay through a small die.
Available from craft and art stores

Degasser

Vacuum chamber pot that removes air bubbles from silicone mixtures prior to pouring into a mould. Not necessary for small batches of silicone.
Available online and from specialist mould suppliers

Dental alginate

Powder alginate, similar to that used in life casting but specifically designed for use in the mouth to take impressions of teeth.
Available at specialist dental suppliers and The Monster Makers online store.

Dental articulator

Device used by dentists to hold upper and lower teeth casts in the natural 'biting' position. This is useful if you are sculpting teeth with fangs as they can be fitted together to be more comfortable for the performer.
Available from online auction sites

Fine-pored sponge

Red sponge with a fine texture used to stipple Pros-Aide cream over the edge of appliances to make the edge invisible.
Available from make-up suppliers

Fixer spray

Used to seal the back of gelatine appliances and painted surfaces. Kryolan Fixing Spray, Ben Nye Final Seal and Green Marble Sealer are recommended brands.
Available from specialist make-up suppliers

Foam latex

Soft lightweight sponge-like material used for making prosthetic appliances. Pre-made foam latex pieces are available from RBFX Studios and other online suppliers

Fumed silica

Lightweight filler used as a thicker. When mixed with Pros-Aide adhesive it creates a thick product that can be applied as an edge filler on prosthetic pieces. Extremely dangerous to breathe in when in its powder form, so wear a dust mask.
Available from specialist make-up and mould-making suppliers.

Gelatine

Granular substance from animal derivatives used to make realistic translucent prosthetic appliances. 300 Bloom is best for prosthetic appliances. You can also purchase it in small packets and sheets from supermarkets, but these are only useful for small burn effects and wounds.
Available from make-up suppliers and grocery stores

Glycerine

Clear, colourless, viscous liquid that, when mixed with sorbitol and gelatine granules, improves the structure and texture of the set gelatine.
Available online and in craft/candle-making stores

Isopropyl alcohol (IPA)

Also known as 99% alcohol. Used to activate alcohol ink palettes and dissolve adhesives.
Available in some drug stores/chemists, chemical suppliers and make-up FX suppliers

Isopropyl myristate

Composed of isopropyl alcohol and myristic acid. It breaks down prosthetic adhesive and is often used to aid prosthetic removal.
Available from make-up suppliers and online

Lighter fluid (or Naptha)

Used to smooth oil-based clays. Highly flammable. Always use a respirator.
Available from supermarkets and hardware stores

Mixing skip

Large flexible tub used to mix plaster. The flexibility allows for easier clean up when the plaster dries.
Available from hardware or craft stores

Mold Max 30

Tin-cured silicone rubber compound with exceptional working properties and library life (storage). It also possesses a slightly longer cure time. Useful for mould making. Since this is a tin-based silicone it cannot be used to manufacture platinum silicone appliances, as tin inhibits the cure of platinum silicone.
Available from Smooth-On

Monster Clay

Specially designed sculpting medium to sculpt maquettes and prosthetics. It is very versatile and can be heated and poured into moulds. It comes in a variety of hardnesses.
Available at most sculpting suppliers and make-up effects shops, specifically from The Monster Makers online

OOMOO 25 & 30

Easy to use silicone rubber compounds that feature convenient one-to-one by volume mix ratios (no scales necessary). They don't need degassing and are useful for mould making.
Available online from Smooth-on and mould-making suppliers

Petroleum jelly

Used as a protective barrier and to prevent certain materials sticking to themselves. It is also popular as a mould release for plaster and silicone. Vaseline is a popular brand.
Available at drug stores/chemists

Plaster

Porous material used to make moulds. It comes in powder form and is mixed with water to activate it. When it goes though the curing stage it heats up. The principal types are:

Hydrocal: a fast-setting plaster that is good for life casts and general mould making;
UltraCal 30: sets slower, is stronger, can withstand heat and is used to make foam latex pieces;
Herculite no. 2: a very hard plaster available in the UK as an alternative to UltraCal;
Dental stone: an expensive plaster used to create very durable casts of teeth. UltraCal 30 can also be used for this purpose;
Plaster of Paris: a very weak brittle plaster generally unsuitable for mould making.
Available at mould-making suppliers and some make-up effects shops

Plaster bandage

Gauze bandage impregnated with plaster. When wet and squeezed out the plaster activates. Plaster bandage is a useful tool in mould making as it quickly dries to a rigid form and can be used to support the alginate on life casts.
Available from medical suppliers, mould and casting suppliers and some make-up FX shops

PlatSil 7315

A platinum silicone that cures to a glass-clear finish. Particularly useful for making transparent moulds for Pros-Aide transfers. It's one of the more expensive silicones and is mostly used for small two-dimensional transfers.
Available from Mouldlife

PlatSil Gel 10

Two-part platinum-based silicone used to make facial prosthetics. Latex can inhibit the cure to this material so use vinyl gloves and keep away from uncured foam and liquid latex. Smith's Prosthetic Deadener can be added to alter the softness of the cured silicone and help make more realistic prosthetics.
Available at Mouldlife. Smooth-On has an equivalent product called Dragon Skin

Pros-Aide

Contact adhesive used to stick most prosthetic materials. Also used to make PAX, a paint for foam latex. It comes in both liquid form, as Pros-Aide 2 (less sticky for making PAX), and cream (useful to hand-lay hair). The cream can also be mixed with fumed silica to make edge filler.
Available from make-up FX suppliers

Powder puff

Velour-covered padding, usually in the shape of a disc, used to press powder into a make-up to eliminate shine.
Available from make-up suppliers

Rasp

Metal-toothed tool used to smooth out the plaster mould.
Available from hardware stores

Rubber mixing bowls

Small flexible bowls used to mix small batches of plaster and alginate. Their flexibility allows for easier clean-up.
Available from make-up hardware and craft stores

Scales

Used to measure materials, particularly silicone. Digital scales are best.
Available in supermarkets and kitchen supply shops

Silicone pigment

Highly pigmented colour added to any type of clear silicone in order to tint it to the desired colour. Can be used to colour silicone for appliances as well as for mould making.
Available from mould-making suppliers

Sorbitol

Food-grade humectant liquid added to gelatine granules, along with glycerine, to improve the structure of the gelatine.
Available from make-up and mould-making suppliers

Stipple sponge

Coarse black sponge made from reticulated foam. Used to create scabs with fake blood. It is also useful as a sculpting tool to create skin pores and texture on clay sculpts.
Available from make-up suppliers

Telesis 5 adhesive and Telesis 5 thinner
Medical-grade adhesive used to stick most appliance materials. It can be thinned with Telesis 5 thinner to enable edges to be re-lifted, making repositioning easier.
Available from make-up suppliers

TinThix
A thickener that, when added to silicone, allows you to 'butter' the mixture on appliances when mould making.
Available from mould-making suppliers

Tongue depressor
Wooden stick used to mix materials.
Available from make-up and mould-making suppliers

Translucent powder
Fine powder used to eliminate the shine of PAX paint without altering the colour. Can also be used to mark out the edges of appliances to indicate glue placement.
Available from make-up suppliers

Ultra 4 epoxy parfilm
Spray mould release used on silicone and epoxy moulds.
Available from make-up and mould-making suppliers

Water clay
Water-based clay that dries out and becomes brittle when left exposed. Mostly used for building clay walls in mould making.
Available at art and mould-making suppliers

INDEX